SMALLMOUTH BASS

THE HUNTING & FISHING LIBRARY™

By Dick Sternberg

DICK STERNBERG learned to catch smallmouth as a youngster fishing small midwestern streams. Since then, he has explored many of the continent's premier smallmouth waters, from Basswood Lake, Ontario, to Dale Hollow Lake, Tennessee. During his years as a professional biologist, he had ample opportunity to study smallmouth behavior, especially in big rivers. His broad base of experience will help you gain a better understanding of smallmouth habits and modern fishing techniques.

CY DECOSSE INCORPORATED
Chairman: Cy DeCosse
President: James B. Maus
Executive Vice President: William B. Jones

SMALLMOUTH BASS
Author and Project Director: Dick Sternberg
Editor: Parker Bauer
Art Directors: Bradley Springer, William B. Jones
Project Manager: Teresa Marrone
Researchers: Joseph Cella, Jeff Howard, Dave McCormack, James Moynagh
Consultants: Tony Bean, Greg Bohn, John Herrick, Don Lamont, Glenn Lau, Ralph Manns, Karl Maslowski, Steve Serns, Rich Zaleski
Technical Photo Director: Joseph Cella
Principal Photographer: William Lindner
Contributing Photographers: Mark Barrett, Des and Jen Bartlett/Bruce Coleman Inc., Jeffrey Baylis, Tony Bean, Dave Bishop, Les Blacklock, William Damon, Daniel Halsey, The In-Fisherman, Lefty Kreh, Janet Mason, Roger Peterson, William Pflieger, Steve Price, Jerry Robb, Doug Stamm, Dick Sternberg, Dan Sura, Jim Tuten, Don Wirth
Lake and River Illustrations: Jon Q. Wright
Boat Control Illustrations: Thomas Boll
Production and Print Production Management: Jim Bindas, Julie Churchill, Christine Watkins
Production Staff: Yelena Konrardy, Carol McMall, Lisa Rosenthal, Dave Schelitzche, Linda Schloegel, Jennie Smith, Delores Swanson, Bryan Trandem, Nik Wogstad

Cooperating Agencies and Individuals: Carter Allan, Arkansas Dept. of Game and Fish; Alumacraft Boat Co. — Bob Hobson, Roger McGregor; Arctic Cat Snowmobiles; B.A.S.S. — Dave Nunley, John Riley, Tommy Thorpe; Larry Belusz, Missouri Dept. of Conservation; Berkley & Company, Inc. — Ben Alspach, Rick Kalsow; Rick Berry; Peter Borque, Maine Dept. of Fisheries; Burger Brothers Sporting Goods; California Dept. of Fish and Game — Charles von Geldern, Don Whiteline; Ray Carignan; Glenn Carr, Pro Anglers Inc.; Homer Circle; Dr. Sheryl Coombs, Parmly Hearing Institute; Jack Dallman, Yar-Craft, Inc.; Chuck DeNoto; Lisa Dougherty, Fenwick-Woodstream Corp.; Frankie Dusenka, Frankie's Live Bait; Don Emitt, CarByDon Mfg.; Ferguson-Keller Associates, Inc.; Bill Fletcher, Livingston Boat Dock; Dr. Calvin Fremling, Winona State University; Butch Furtman; Dave Golden, *Ontario Outdoors*; Mike Grupa, Stearns Manufactufing Co.; Dick Grzywinski; Herrick Enterprises-Wave Wackers; Dave Hughes; Grant and Judy Hughes, Muskego Point Resort; Bill Huntley; *The In-Fisherman* — Dave Csanda, Doug Stange, Dan Sura; Rick James; Johnson Fishing, Inc.-Minn Kota Trolling Motors; Michael Jones, Stren Fishing Line; Ray Juetten, Michigan Dept. of Natural Resources; Ernie Kilpatrick; Bruce Kirschner, Sage- Winslow Mfg. Corp.; Dr. Weldon Larimore, Illinois Natural History Survey; Fred Leckie, West Virginia Dept. of Natural Resources; Leroy's Minnows; Lindy-Little Joe; Malcolm Lipsey, Morris Ferry Dock; Doug Loehr; Dick McCleskey, New Mexico Dept. of Natural Resources; Mercury Marine/Mariner Outboards — Stan Bular, Jim Kalkofen, Clem Koehler; Dr. Rudolph Miller, Oklahoma State University; Minnesota Dept. of Natural Resources — Gary Barnard, Larry Gates, Gary Grunwald, Mark Heywood, Duane Shodeen; Mister Twister, Inc.; Jim Moore, Lund American, Inc.; Jeff Murray; Tom Neustrom; New York State Dept. of Environmental Conservation — Pat Festa, Bob Lange; Bill Nichols; Terry Niedenfuer, ABW, Inc.; Tony Nigro; Normark Corporation; Ohio Dept. of Natural Resources — Carl Baker, Jim Schoby; Pat Olson; Ontario Ministry of Natural Resources — Terry Hicks, Jim MacLean, Gordon Pyzer, Dr. Richard Ryder, Les Sztramko, Lloyd Thurston; Vaughn Paragamian, Iowa Conservation Commission; Dr. Gile Pauly, University of Washington; Dave Peterson; William Pflieger, Missouri Dept. of Conservation; Floyd Preas; Steve Price; R&R Marine; Mike Radulovich; Nancy Raffeto, University of Wisconsin; Buzz Ramsey, Luhr Jensen and Sons, Inc.; Ed Rezak, Kala Enterprises, Inc.; Jim Rivers; Tom Rodgers, *Smallmouth Inc.*; Frank Ryck, Missouri Dept. of Conservation; Dan Schuber, Virginia Commission of Game and Inland Fisheries; Bill Scifres, The Indianapolis Star; Si-Tex Marine Electronics, Inc. — Dave Church, Jack Phillips; Thayne Smith, Lowrance Electronics, Inc.; Jack Sokol & Associates, Inc.; Edwin Sox; Howard Steere, Orvis; Stinger Tackle Company; Strike Master, Inc.; Suzuki Outboards — Dick Dolan, Frank Wright; Tommy Tenpenny; Texas Parks and Wildlife Dept. — Nick Carter, Phil Durocher; Trilene Fishing Line; Tru-Turn, Inc.; Chuck Tryon, Maxima; Harry Turner, The Outdoorsman; Umpqua Feather Merchants; Dr. James Underhill, University of Minnesota; Vados Live Bait and Tackle; Lou Vogele; Rick Wayne; Billy Westmorland; Bill White; Don Wirth
Color Separations: La Cromolito
Printing: W.A. Krueger Company (1286)

Also available from the publisher: *The Art of Freshwater Fishing, Cleaning & Cooking Fish, Fishing With Live Bait, Largemouth Bass, Panfish, The Art of Hunting, Fishing With Artificial Lures, Walleye*

Library of Congress Catalog Card Number 86-16617
ISBN 0-86573-017-2
ISBN 0-86573-018-0 (pbk.)

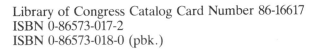

Distributed by Prentice Hall Press
A Division of Simon & Schuster, Inc., New York, NY
ISBN 0-13-813163-5 (hbk.)

Contents

Introduction 5

Equipment 7
    Rods, Reels & Line 8
    Boats, Motors & Accessories 12
    Electronics 16
    Wading Gear 17

Understanding the Smallmouth 19
    Smallmouth Bass Basics 20
    Senses 22
    Habitat Preferences 24
    Feeding & Growth 28
    Competition 30
    How Weather Affects Smallmouth .32
    Spawning Behavior 36
    Homing 38

Where to Find Smallmouth 41
    How to Select Smallmouth Waters .42
    Where to Find Smallmouth Through the Seasons 49
    Mesotrophic Lakes 50
    Oligotrophic Lakes 54
    Eutrophic Lakes 58
    Pits 59
    Mid-Depth Reservoirs 60
    Shallow Reservoirs 64
    Canyon Reservoirs 65
    Small to Medium-Sized Rivers 66
    Big Rivers 68
    Prime Smallmouth Waters 70

Basic Smallmouth-Fishing Techniques .79
    Smallmouth-Fishing Fundamentals 80
    Boat Control 82
    How to Play a Smallmouth 86
    Fishing with Artificial Lures 88
    Fishing with Live Bait 114

Techniques for Special Situations 125
    Fishing During the Spawning Period 126
    Smallmouth in the Weeds 128
    Smallmouth in Woody Cover 133
    Manmade Features 136
    Smallmouth in Rocks & Boulders 138
    River Fishing 141
    Low-Clarity Water 146
    Ultra-Clear Water 147
    Night Fishing for Smallmouth 148
    Trophy Smallmouth 150
    Ice Fishing for Smallmouth 154

Index 156

Introduction

The smallmouth bass could be called the perfect gamefish. A willing biter, it is quick to strike an artificial lure and equally quick to make a spectacular leap and throw the hook. Although it is an excellent table fish, many anglers place such a high value on its sporting qualities that they release any smallmouth they catch.

In lightly fished waters, catching smallmouth is not much of a challenge. In remote regions of the northern states and Canada, for instance, anglers routinely bag dozens of smallmouth a day. But in waters where angling pressure is more intense, fishing is a lot tougher. Populations have been fished down to the point where all of the "dumb" smallmouth have been caught. And the smallmouth that remain have more living space and more food, so they are more difficult to find and catch.

To locate smallmouth, today's angler must be well versed in smallmouth behavior and seasonal movement patterns. To make them bite, he must be familiar with a wide variety of live-bait and artificial-lure techniques.

Chapter 1, "Equipment," shows you what to look for when selecting rods, reels and line; boats and motors; electronics; and even waders. Some fishermen make the mistake of purchasing expensive but useless equipment, thinking it will miraculously improve their fishing. This chapter will tell you what equipment you need — and what you don't need.

Chapter 2, "Understanding the Smallmouth," shows you what makes smallmouth tick. You'll learn about their spawning habits, how they detect danger, the type of habitat they prefer, what they eat and how weather affects them. We'll also show you how different levels of competition in different waters can alter the smallmouth's behavior, and how these differences affect your fishing strategy.

Chapter 3, "Where to Find Smallmouth," is a quick reference for locating smallmouth in every type of water. Whether you fish in natural lakes, manmade lakes, or rivers, this chapter will show you exactly where to find smallmouth in each season of the year. We've added a new feature to this volume of The Hunting & Fishing Library, a guide to premier fishing waters in North America. This thoroughly researched guide will put you on the smallmouth in a hurry and save a lot of wasted trips.

Chapter 4, "Basic Smallmouth-Fishing Techniques," describes every live-bait and artificial-lure technique a smallmouth angler needs to know, from bobber-fishing with leeches to fly fishing with bass bugs. Many smallmouth fishermen tend to get in a rut — they use the same bait and technique regardless of the type of water or time of year. By familiarizing yourself with the techniques in this chapter, you will become a much more versatile angler.

Chapter 5, "Techniques for Special Situations," takes you way beyond the basics. You'll see how the experts can turn tough or unusual fishing conditions into a smallmouth bonanza. We'll show you an assortment of little-known techniques and tips that will help you snake smallmouth from weeds and brush, and irritate them into biting around spawning time. You'll discover how to bag trophy-sized fish, how to take advantage of the smallmouth's aggressive nighttime habits, even how to catch smallmouth through the ice, something that most fishermen consider impossible.

Anyone who picks up this book is sure to be attracted by the beautiful full-color photography. But it is much more than a picture book. It contains more facts on smallmouth bass than have ever been assembled under one cover. The major contributors, like Rich Zaleski from Connecticut, Tony Bean from Tennessee, and John Herrick from Minnesota, rank among the country's leading smallmouth anglers. This wealth of information, more than the average angler could unearth in a lifetime, will eliminate most of those days when the fish just won't cooperate.

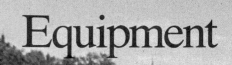

Rods, Reels & Line

GENERAL-PURPOSE OUTFIT. A 5¼- to 5¾-foot medium-power, fast-action spinning rod with matching reel suits the majority of smallmouth-fishing situations. When spooled with 6- to 8-pound mono, this outfit will handle lures weighing from 1/16 to 5/8 ounce.

For maximum sport, smallmouth fishermen should use the lightest rod and reel that suits the conditions. A light outfit not only makes the most of the smallmouth's magnificent fighting qualities, but is easier to cast for long periods of time, and is ideal for tossing the small lures and baits that smallmouth usually prefer. The only reason for using heavy tackle is to fish in timber, brush or other snaggy cover, or to troll or cast large lures.

RODS. Experienced smallmouth fishermen carry several rods, each intended for a different fishing situation. This way, they are prepared to use a variety of lures and baits, and do not waste time rerigging every time they try a new presentation.

The photos on pages 8 to 11 show the most popular smallmouth-fishing outfits. You may need a different type of rod for some of the special situations shown later in this book. For instance, an 8- to 8½-foot spinning rod makes it easier to unsnag your lure from a rocky bottom (pages 138-139).

If you do not wish to carry several outfits, your best choice is the general-purpose outfit shown at left. It has its drawbacks for fishing with live bait or heavy lures, but is the best compromise for most smallmouth fishing.

Smallmouth do not necessarily take a lure or bait as vigorously as they fight, so any rod you select should be sensitive enough to detect subtle strikes. Most experts prefer graphite or boron rods. Their stiffness makes them very sensitive and enables you to set the hook fast and hard. But most manufacturers no longer make boron rods because improvements in the quality of graphite have resulted in rods that are less expensive and just as sensitive. Some high-quality fiberglass rods will also do the job.

Before buying a graphite rod, check its actual graphite content. If this information is not readily available, it can usually be obtained from the manufacturer. For good sensitivity, a rod should have a graphite content of at least 80 percent. All graphite rods are composites and contain at least a small percentage of fiberglass. Some rods advertised as graphite actually have a graphite content of 10 percent or less.

REELS. The most important consideration in selecting a spinning reel for smallmouth fishing is a smooth, reliable drag. Many fishermen make the mistake of buying a cheap spinning reel to save a few dollars. The first time they hook a good-sized smallmouth, the drag malfunctions and the smallmouth snaps the line.

The only sure way to test a drag is to spool line on the reel, then pull on it to be sure it comes off smoothly. If you cannot test the drag this way, check to see how much adjustment is required to go from a light drag setting to a heavy one. Generally, the best drags are those with the largest amount of adjustment between settings.

Another consideration is the gear ratio. A reel with a high gear ratio, about 5:1, enables you to retrieve lures rapidly and take up slack line when a smallmouth suddenly changes direction. But a high gear ratio is not the best choice for retrieving lures with a lot of water resistance. The handle is harder to turn, so your wrist and arm tire more quickly. A gear ratio of about 4:1 will solve the problem.

Many spinning reels have small-diameter spools which make the reel light and compact. But a small spool causes the mono to come off in tight coils. Casting will be difficult and the line may catch on the spool when a smallmouth runs with your bait. The problem is less severe with light, limp mono than with stiff, heavy mono, which has more *memory,* or tendency to remain coiled.

Baitcasting reels should also have a smooth drag. A free-spool model with a magnetic brake system minimizes the problem of backlashing, especially when casting light lures into the wind.

A button to disengage the anti-reverse is also a good feature in a baitcasting reel. Most baitcasting reels have a built-in anti-reverse. The handle will not turn backward, so you must rely on the drag when a smallmouth makes a run. But if you can disengage the anti-reverse, you can thumb the reel instead of

LIVE-BAIT OUTFIT. A 6- to 7-foot, light-power, soft- to medium-action spinning rod with matching reel flexes enough so you can cast without tearing the bait off the hook. And the fish will not feel resistance when it swims off with the bait.

HEAVY CASTING-TROLLING OUTFIT. A 5½- to 6-foot, medium-power, fast-action baitcasting rod with matching reel works well for casting or trolling heavy or water-resistant lures. Baitcasting gear also allows you to thumb the spool for pinpoint casting accuracy.

FLY-FISHING OUTFIT. A 7-weight, 8½-foot fly rod and single-action reel spooled with 7-weight floating line allows you to cast anything from a delicate dry fly to a bulky bass bug. For special-purpose fly tackle, refer to the recommendations on pages 108 to 111.

relying on the drag. This way, your line will not break because the drag malfunctions.

The fly reel you select should have enough capacity for your fly line and at least 50 yards of 12- to 20-pound dacron backing. Select a sturdy, single-action reel balanced to your rod. The reel should have interchangeable spools so you can easily switch from floating to sink-tip or sinking lines.

LINE. Smallmouth anglers rely almost exclusively on monofilament line. Be sure to select premium-grade monofilament because cheap mono has weak spots caused by an inconsistent diameter.

Light line is best in most situations. It lets you cast farther, allows your lure to run deeper without restricting its action (page 102), and makes it easier to feel bites. But there are some drawbacks. You cannot set the hook as hard, you cannot cast heavy lures, and you must be more careful when fighting the fish. Unless you are fishing in heavy cover or on a snaggy bottom, you will seldom need line heavier than 8-pound test.

Another advantage to light line is its low visibility. In clear water, you will probably get twice as many strikes with 4-pound line as you would with 10-pound line.

Premium-grade monofilament is less visible than cheap mono of the same strength, because it has a smaller diameter. And clear or green-tinted line is much less visible than fluorescent line.

Although low-visibility line is an advantage in clear water, you may have difficulty detecting subtle strikes because you cannot see the line twitch. If the water clarity is low, use fluorescent line. It is not visible to the fish, and is much easier for you to see.

Limp monofilament is usually the best choice. It is easier to cast than stiffer line, and because it flexes more, your lures will have better action. But limp mono has a softer finish, so it scratches more easily, especially when you fish in rocks, timber, brush or tough-stemmed weeds. In these types of cover, stiff, abrasion-resistant mono is a better choice.

Most brands of limp mono have a high stretch factor. Some stretch as much as 30 percent. A high stretch factor makes it more difficult to detect strikes and set the hook. If your fishing technique requires a long line, then stiff, low-stretch mono would be a better choice.

Floating and sink-tip fly lines from 6 to 8 weight are recommended for most smallmouth fishing. Lines with weight-forward tapers cast the large, wind-resistant flies used for smallmouth more easily than double-tapers or level lines.

Tips for Selecting and Using Rods, Reels and Line

SELECT a level-wind reel with the handle on the left for flippin' or dabbling (page 135). This way, a right-handed fisherman can drop his line into a likely spot and begin reeling without switching hands.

CHOOSE a one-piece rod with a graphite handle for maximum sensitivity. The tapered construction insures that the impulse of a strike is transferred directly to your hand rather than absorbed by a cork or rubber grip.

TEST the action of a rod by stringing it, then observing the bend while pulling on the line. A fast-action rod (above) bends mainly at the tip. A medium-action rod starts bending at the middle; while a slow-action rod bends over its entire length.

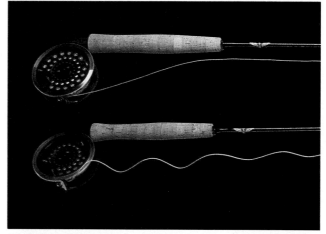

SPOOL enough dacron backing on your fly reel so the line comes within ⅛ to ¼ inch of the pillars when the reel is filled (top). Without backing, the line forms tight coils because the spool diameter is too small (bottom). The coils make casting more difficult.

Fishing Qualities of Various Types of Line

TYPE	STRETCH	ABRASION RESISTANCE	MEMORY	DIAMETER	VISIBILITY	KNOT STRENGTH
Limp Mono	high[1]	low	low	low	*	high
Stiff Mono	medium	high	medium	high	*	medium
Cofilament[2]	low	low	high	medium	high	low

[1] Some premium grades of limp mono have a medium stretch factor.
[2] Consists of a low-stretch polyester core surrounded by a nylon sheath.
* Depends on color of line.
Note: Information in this chart is the result of tests conducted by Hunting & Fishing Library researchers.

BASS BOATS are the standard on big southern reservoirs, which may be a hundred miles long. To cover this distance, anglers use outboards up to 150 horsepower, attaining speeds over 60 mph. Bass boats are gaining popularity in the North, but the low-profile hull is not well-suited to the rough water on large northern lakes.

Boats, Motors & Accessories

Depending on the type of water you fish, the best craft for smallmouth may be a high-powered bass boat, an aluminum or fiberglass semi-V, a jon boat, or a canoe. Smallmouth anglers who fish a variety of waters often have two or three boats.

BASS BOATS. These boats provide the ultimate in fishing comfort and convenience. Because of their fiberglass construction and tri-hull design, they are very stable, so you can safely stand up while casting. If you prefer to sit, the sides are low enough that you do not have to hold your rod up when retrieving.

Most bass boats have an elevated front casting deck, a carpeted floor to muffle sound, an aerated live well, rod- and gear-storage compartments, a bow-mounted trolling motor, and a flasher set up for high-speed sounding.

SEMI-V BOATS. The term *semi-V* indicates that the boat has a V-shaped bow, but a relatively flat bottom at the stern. The V-shaped bow serves to part the waves, and the flat bottom makes the boat stable. There are two basic types of semi-Vs: aluminum and fiberglass.

Aluminum semi-Vs are light, so the bow rides up on the waves instead of cutting through them, resulting in a rough ride. Fiberglass semi-Vs are heavier, so they ride more smoothly and are less affected by wind. They are also quieter than aluminum, but are less durable and more expensive.

Most smallmouth fishermen prefer a semi-V with tiller steering. A tiller gives you much better boat control than a steering wheel, especially for back-trolling (page 83). Other desirable equipment includes a flasher and a transom-mounted electric

ALUMINUM SEMI-Vs are the favorite on northern lakes. Most fishermen use 14- to 16-footers equipped with 10- to 50-horsepower outboards. The V-shaped bow of these boats makes them quite seaworthy, and their light weight makes it possible to get them in and out of the water at even the poorest boat landings.

trolling motor. Some of the more expensive semi-Vs come equipped with bass-boat features like live wells, carpeted floors, air-pedestal seats and elevated casting decks.

JON BOATS. The stability and light weight of a jon boat make it ideal for river fishing. Many rivers lack developed boat landings, but a pair of fishermen can easily carry a 14-foot jon boat to the water. A 6-horsepower outboard provides all the power you will normally need. With a 16-foot jon boat, most anglers use a 10- to 15-horsepower outboard.

Some fishermen rig their jon boats with a bow-mounted trolling motor, flasher and live well. But others would rather go light. They rely solely on their outboard, check the depth visually or with a push pole, and keep their fish in a cooler.

CANOES. Anglers who regularly fish difficult-to-reach waters prefer aluminum canoes. They are inexpensive, durable, and light enough for one person to carry on his shoulders when portaging around dangerous rapids or from one lake to another. Be-

cause of the light weight, they are easy to paddle long distances.

Like fiberglass semi-Vs, fiberglass canoes are heavier than aluminum ones, so the wind does not blow them around as easily. The extra weight also makes them less tippy. When a fiberglass canoe scrapes on rocks, it makes a lot less noise than an aluminum canoe and is not as likely to spook fish.

Most canoe fishermen travel light; the only extra equipment is a portable flasher, paddles, and an anchor rope. For an anchor, they tie on a rock.

Where motors are permitted, use a square-stern canoe (opposite page) or one with a bracket for mounting a motor alongside the stern. A side-mount bracket will usually take a 2- to 4-horsepower outboard. If you prefer, you can attach a transom-mount electric motor to the stern or to the side-mount bracket. With an ordinary canoe, you can simply attach the electric motor to the gunwale. Even a small electric motor will push a canoe at a surprising speed.

FIBERGLASS SEMI-Vs are becoming popular on big lakes because the hull is flared at the bow to deflect waves to the side. Without the flared bow, spray flies up and the wind blows it back into the boat. Fiberglass semi-Vs used for smallmouth fishing range from 15 to 17 feet and are normally rigged with 35- to 55-horsepower motors.

JON BOATS are the ultimate craft for river fishing. Because they draw only a few inches of water, they will float over shallow, rocky stretches. And should they scrape bottom, the aluminum hull will not be damaged. A jon boat's flat-bottom design gives it excellent side-to-side stability.

CANOES are the only craft practical for long-distance portaging or fishing in wilderness areas where access is difficult and motors are often banned. Canoes also work well for fishing rivers with rocky riffles or whitewater stretches.

SQUARE-STERN CANOES are wide and deep; they carry a lot of gear and take motors up to 10 horsepower.

Electronics

A flasher is an indispensable tool for most types of smallmouth fishing. It enables you to find likely structure quickly, and if you know how to interpret the signal, you can even check the bottom type and determine if fish are present.

Because most smallmouth fishing is done in relatively shallow water, your flasher should have a scale of about 0 to 20 or 0 to 30 feet. This way, the signal is spread over a large portion of the dial so it is easy to read. If you also fish in deep water, choose a flasher with a scale that can be switched to 0 to 60 or 0 to 100 feet. Your flasher should also have a suppressor, either manual or built in, to reduce interference from your outboard or from other electronic units operating nearby.

Graph recorders and LCRs (liquid-crystal recorders) further refine the signal by printing it on paper or a screen. Most smallmouth experts prefer a graph recorder to an LCR because the printout is much clearer and easier to interpret.

A good selection of depth ranges and a suppressor are also important when selecting a graph. Other desirable features include a paper-speed adjustment so you can run the paper faster in shallow water and slower in deep water, a light for night fishing, and a grayline adjustment to help you discriminate fish from bottom.

If you prefer an LCR, select one with a lot of *pixels,* the small squares that make up the image. The more pixels, the sharper the image will be. To avoid blocky fish marks, the unit should have at least 1,000 pixels per square inch and preferably 2,000. A model with a zoom feature gives extra detail because you can zoom in to enlarge the image. Some of the better LCRs have a grayline feature, much like a graph.

Another electronic device that can improve smallmouth fishing success is a surface-temperature gauge. This device is most valuable in spring because it can help you locate the warmwater zones where smallmouth are likely to spawn.

Most of the experienced smallmouth fishermen we have interviewed do not use pH meters or electronic color selectors. There is no scientific evidence to indicate that smallmouth have any specific pH preference or that they are triggered to strike by the colors the selector recommends.

Tips on Selecting Electronics

COLOR FLASHERS make it easier to tell small fish from large ones. Orange marks on this model are baitfish; red marks, smallmouth bass.

GRAPH vs. LCR. A graph (left) shows a small fish above bottom and a big fish near bottom. The dark signal is a rocky reef. On the LCR (right), the same small fish is a tiny square; the larger one a bump on bottom. The rocky reef is not as evident as on the graph.

Wading Gear

A great deal of smallmouth fishing is done by wading in small streams. For this type of fishing, you will need a good pair of chest waders or hip boots.

The major considerations in buying waders or hip boots are the type of leg material and the type of sole. Most wading gear used in smallmouth fishing is made of rubber or nylon. It pays to buy high-quality rubber rather than cheap rubber wading gear. High-quality rubber is very durable; cheap rubber will probably tear or develop leaks after you wear it a few times. Nylon wading gear is lighter and less expensive, but may not be quite as durable as high-quality rubber.

For wading on slippery rocks, choose waders or hip boots with felt soles. Or, glue pieces of felt or carpet to your soles (see below). Rubber soles are fine for sandy or muddy bottoms.

Another consideration in buying waders is whether to select a boot-foot model or a stocking-foot model with separate wading boots. Stocking-foot waders are less bulky, so you can wade more easily in current. But the thin nylon uppers snag and rip more easily.

Tips for Using Waders and Hip Boots

CUT pieces of felt to fit your soles and heels, then attach them with shoe-repair cement. You will have good traction, even on slippery rocks.

SPRINKLE the inside of rubber waders or hip boots with baby powder to make them slide on easily. Powder removes the sticky texture.

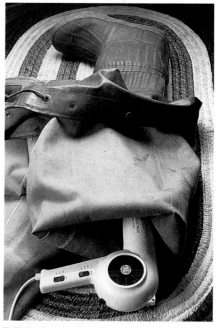

DRY damp waders or hip boots using a hair dryer. Set the dryer on low heat, then let it blow into each leg for 10 to 15 minutes.

Understanding the Smallmouth

Smallmouth Bass Basics

Known for its aerial acrobatics and never-give-up determination, the smallmouth bass has a well-deserved reputation as the fightingest freshwater gamefish. After a smallmouth strikes, it usually makes a sizzling run for the surface, does a cartwheel in an attempt to throw the hook, then wages a dogged battle in deep water.

The smallmouth bass, *Micropterus dolomieui,* was originally found mainly in the eastern United States. Its range extended from northern Minnesota to southern Quebec on the north, and from northern Georgia to eastern Oklahoma on the south. It was not found east of the Appalachians. But owing to its tremendous popularity, the smallmouth has been widely stocked and is now found in every state with the exceptions of Florida, Louisiana and Alaska. It has also been stocked in most Canadian provinces and in Asia, Africa, Europe and South America.

The smallmouth is sometimes called *bronzeback* because of the bronze reflections from its scales. Other common names include black bass, brown bass, Oswego bass, redeye and green trout.

Like its close relatives the largemouth and spotted bass, the smallmouth belongs to the sunfish family. Smallmouth have been known to hybridize naturally with spotted bass, and biologists have created a smallmouth-largemouth hybrid nicknamed the *meanmouth* because of its aggressive nature.

APPEARANCE of smallmouth (top) differs from that of spotted bass (lower left) and largemouth (lower right). Smallmouth have nine dark vertical bars that come and go, and three bars radiating from the eye. Smallmouth lack the dark horizontal band present on largemouth and spotted bass, and normally have a darker belly. On spotted bass, the horizontal band consists of a row of diamond-shaped dark spots. They may have several rows of spots below the band. The band on largemouth lacks the diamond-shaped spots.

Although smallmouth bass are considered excellent eating, the modern trend in sport fishing is toward catch-and-release, especially in heavily fished waters. Where fishing pressure is heavy, the large smallmouth are quickly removed, leaving only the small ones. Catch-and-release fishing is the best solution to this problem.

Smallmouth Bass Range

On July 9, 1955, D.L. Hayes was trolling a pearl-colored Bomber around a shale point in Dale Hollow Lake, Kentucky. At about 10:00 a.m. he hooked a huge fish, and after a 20-minute fight landed what turned out to be the world-record smallmouth. It weighed 11 pounds, 15 ounces and was 27 inches long.

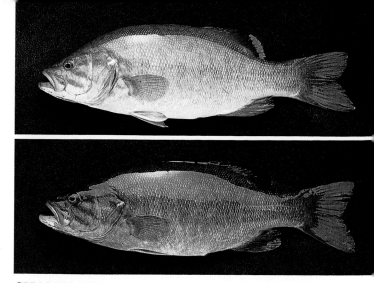

CHAMELEON EFFECT is shown by these two photos of the same smallmouth. The top photo was taken after the fish had been held in a light-colored tank; the bottom photo after it had been held in a dark-colored tank.

MOUTH SIZE clearly separates smallmouth bass (top) from largemouth bass (bottom). On a smallmouth, the upper jaw extends to the middle of the eye; on a largemouth, beyond the rear of the eye. The mouth of a spotted bass is intermediate in size.

Basswood Lake, Ont. (slightly bog stained)

Lake George, N.Y. (very clear)

Percy Priest Lake, Tenn. (greenish)

COLOR PHASE of smallmouth bass varies greatly in different waters, depending mainly on the color of the water. These photos show three of the many possible color phases. In murky waters, smallmouth often have pale, grayish coloration.

Senses

To find food and escape danger, smallmouth rely on eyesight to a far greater degree than any of their other senses. As a result, good smallmouth fishermen generally use lures with a natural look. And they take great pains to avoid being seen by the smallmouth, especially when fishing in clear water.

Little scientific research has been done on the smallmouth's sensory capabilities, but some conclusions can be drawn based on field observation. For instance, smallmouth evidently have a well-developed lateral-line sense because they can detect lures that produce vibration in water where the visibility is only a few inches. They also have good hearing as evidenced by the fact that they are easily spooked by noise, especially noise that is transmitted directly into the water. Experienced smallmouth fishermen are careful to avoid slamming the live-well lid or dropping the anchor on the floor of the boat.

The sense of smell evidently plays some role in extremely turbid water, but in most other situations it appears to be less important than the other senses. Some smallmouth anglers believe that scent products, particularly crayfish scents, improve their success. But others who have tested scented lures alongside unscented ones have found no difference. Some scent manufacturers claim their products cover up foreign odors, like those of gasoline and human hands. But anglers who have deliberately soaked their lures in gasoline report that these lures catch smallmouth as well as any other lures, whether treated with scent or not.

Studies have shown that smallmouth bass are less line- and lure-wary than largemouth bass, and thus easier to catch. But the degree of wariness varies greatly in different waters, depending mainly on the amount of competition (pages 30-31).

In waters where the smallmouth population is low and food plentiful, smallmouth can be extremely wary. Any sudden movement by a fisherman will scare them into deeper water, where they refuse to bite. The best policy is to keep a low profile and avoid throwing your shadow over the fish.

But if the population is high and food relatively scarce, smallmouth are not as wary and spooking is not as much of a problem. In fact, scuba divers have attracted smallmouth to within a few feet by tapping rocks on their air tanks.

How the Senses of Smallmouth Bass Compare to Those of Other Gamefish *

FISH SPECIES	DAYTIME VISION	NIGHT VISION	LATERAL LINE	SMELL	HEARING
Smallmouth Bass	Excellent	Fair	Good	Fair	Good
Spotted Bass	Excellent	Good	Good	Fair	Good
Largemouth Bass	Good	Fair	Good	Fair	Good
Walleye	Fair	Excellent	Good	Fair	Good
Sauger	Fair	Excellent	Excellent	Fair	Good
Yellow Perch	Good	Poor	Fair	Fair	Fair
Crappie	Good	Good	Fair	Fair	Fair
Bluegill	Excellent	Fair	Fair	Good	Fair
Northern Pike	Excellent	Poor	Good	Poor	Good
Catfish	Fair	Fair	Excellent	Excellent	Excellent

*Ratings determined from a survey of prominent fish physiologists and fisheries biologists.

Habitat Preferences

Smallmouth bass are fish of clear, clean waters. They are equally at home in streams and lakes, but are rarely found in small ponds, lakes shallower than 25 feet, or any water that is continuously murky or polluted.

To locate smallmouth, you should become familiar with their preferences in regard to the following environmental conditions:

TEMPERATURE. During the summer months, smallmouth in northern lakes are usually found at water temperatures from 67° to 71°F and seldom at temperatures above 80°. But smallmouth in south-

ern reservoirs are often found at temperatures of 78° to 84°. This difference can be explained by the fact that the deeper, cooler water in the reservoirs lacks sufficient oxygen in summer.

Laboratory tests have shown that smallmouth prefer a temperature of about 82°F. But most of these tests were conducted using juvenile smallmouth, whose temperature preference is considerably higher than that of the adults.

These findings have great significance for smallmouth fishermen. If you are fishing in shallow water and catching nothing but undersized smallmouth, you may be able to catch bigger ones by fishing several feet deeper.

During the cold months, smallmouth activity drops off. In laboratory studies, smallmouth fed very little at temperatures below 50°F and lay motionless on the bottom at temperatures below 40°. In their natural surroundings, smallmouth respond to temperature in much the same way.

OXYGEN. Smallmouth can tolerate an oxygen level of 2.5 parts per million, while largemouth can survive at 2.0. This slight difference may explain why largemouth are better able to tolerate stagnant water. But neither species fares well at oxygen levels this low. Feeding and growth are severely reduced if the level remains below 5 parts per million for an extended period.

In most smallmouth waters, the oxygen level is adequate throughout the depths that smallmouth prefer. So measuring oxygen levels will not help you locate the fish. But in highly fertile waters, smallmouth may be confined to shallow water in summer because the depths lack sufficient oxygen.

pH. Smallmouth are found in waters with a pH from 5 to 9. Although the best smallmouth populations are usually found where the pH is from 7.9 to 8.1, there is no research to indicate that smallmouth prefer any specific pH level. Canadian researchers found that smallmouth were unable to successfully reproduce at pH levels from 5.5 to 6.0.

Temperature Preferences and Oxygen Requirements of Various Freshwater Fish

SPECIES	PREFERRED SUMMER TEMP.	OXYGEN REQUIRE-MENT*
Smallmouth bass	67-71°F	2.5 ppm
Largemouth bass	68-78°F	2.0 ppm
Bluegill	75-80°F	3.5 ppm
Walleye	65-75°F	4.0 ppm
Northern pike		1.4 ppm
under 7 pounds	65-70°F	
over 7 pounds	50-55°F	
Brook trout	52-56°F	5.0 ppm
Rainbow trout	55-60°F	1.5 ppm
Black bullhead	78-84°F	less than 1 ppm

* Minimum requirement (in parts per million) for long-term survival at summertime temperatures. Oxygen requirements decrease at lower water temperatures.

CURRENT. Smallmouth prefer moderate current, usually in the range of 0.4 to 1.3 feet per second. This range is slower than that preferred by trout, but faster than that favored by largemouth bass. With a little experience, you will be able to recognize the right current speed (page 141).

In most streams, smallmouth are more numerous in pools with noticeable current than in pools where the water is completely slack.

In lakes, smallmouth often concentrate around river mouths or in areas with wind-induced current, such as a trough between two islands or a narrow channel between two major lobes of a lake.

DEPTH. Smallmouth are generally considered fish of the *epilimnion,* the upper layer of water in a lake that is stratified into temperature layers. They are most likely to be found in shallow areas adjacent to deep water. The depths offer smallmouth refuge from intense light and boat traffic.

In waters that have both smallmouth and largemouth, the smallmouth are usually slightly deeper. Generally, smallmouth stay deep enough that they are not visible from the surface.

In spring, summer and early fall, smallmouth are seldom found at depths exceeding 30 feet. But in late fall and winter, they often congregate in tight schools at depths down to 60 feet.

CLARITY. Although smallmouth will tolerate murky water for short periods, they rarely live in water that remains murky year-around. As a rule, waters where the usual visibility is less than 1 foot do not hold substantial smallmouth populations.

If the water is murky in one portion of a lake but clear in another, chances are that smallmouth will be most numerous in the clearer area. Similarly, smallmouth are usually more plentiful in a clear reach of a stream than in a muddy reach. And in extremely fertile lakes, smallmouth bite best in spring, before intense algal blooms cloud the water, and in fall, after the algae has died back.

BOTTOM TYPE. In most waters, smallmouth are found over a bottom consisting of clean rocks or gravel. This type of bottom is usually rich in smallmouth foods including crayfish and larval insects like dragonfly nymphs and hellgrammites. But in lakes where most of the basin consists of rock, smallmouth often prefer sandy shoal areas, especially those with a sparse growth of weeds. The sandy, weedy areas will hold fewer crayfish and insect larvae, but more baitfish.

SPAWNING HABITAT. To spawn successfully, smallmouth need a rock, gravel or hard sand bottom. Nests on silty bottoms are seldom successful. Stream smallmouth nest in light current, but avoid swift current. The best spawning areas have boulders or other large objects to protect one side of the nest. Waters that tend to remain muddy for long periods of time following a heavy rain are not well suited to successful smallmouth spawning. The suspended silt makes it difficult for the male to defend his nest, and silt deposited on the eggs prevents them from absorbing enough oxygen.

COMPETITOR SPECIES. Populations of other species that compete with smallmouth for food, living space or spawning habitat can greatly affect the size of the smallmouth population and the way the smallmouth behave. Compared to most other freshwater gamefish, smallmouth are poor competitors. If a body of water contains a large number of shallow-water predators like largemouth bass (right) or northern pike, chances are it will not support a dense smallmouth population.

Competition with other fish species can be a major factor in determining smallmouth location. Most reservoirs in the mid-South, for instance, have good populations of largemouth and spotted bass. If largemouth are numerous, smallmouth and spotted bass are normally found in the main-lake portion of the reservoir where the water is relatively deep and clear. Largemouth tend to dominate the upper portion where the water is shallower and the clarity lower. Largemouth also concentrate in shallow creek arms and wherever there is weedy or brushy cover. In reservoirs with fewer largemouth, the smallmouth and spotted bass may occupy the upper as well as the lower portion.

Feeding & Growth

If you have ever caught a smallmouth and examined its stomach contents, chances are you found bits and pieces of crayfish. In waters where crayfish are plentiful, they make up at least two-thirds of the smallmouth's diet.

Because crayfish inhabit the same rocky areas that smallmouth do, they make a convenient target for feeding bass. Other important items in the smallmouth's diet include fish, adult and immature insects, and tadpoles.

The diet of smallmouth bass may vary from season to season, depending on the availability of food. In a five-year food-habits study conducted in Nebish Lake, Wisconsin, crayfish made up 83 percent of the smallmouth's diet in September, but only 14 percent in May. Insects made up 34 percent of the diet in May, but only 4 percent in July.

Smallmouth feed very little during cold-water periods. Normally, they begin feeding in spring when the water temperature reaches about 47°F. Food consumption peaks at water temperatures around 78°. When the water temperature drops below 40° in fall, practically no feeding takes place. However, in some high-competition waters (pages 30-31), smallmouth continue to feed through the ice-cover season.

Smallmouth bass differ from most freshwater gamefish in that males and females grow at about the same rate. Smallmouth in lakes and reservoirs usually grow faster and reach a larger size than those in streams. And smallmouth in southern waters generally grow faster than those in the North. The table at right shows how growth rates vary. In Norris Lake, Tennessee, for instance, an age-6 smallmouth measures 18 inches (about 4 pounds); in Lake Opeongo, Ontario, a smallmouth of the same age measures only 12.2 inches (about 1 pound).

Although smallmouth grow much faster in the South, their maximum size varies less from North to South than would be expected. Smallmouth live as long as 18 years in the North, but seldom longer than 7 years in the South. Higher metabolic rates cause faster burnout in southern waters.

Smallmouth weighing up to 11 pounds, 8 ounces have been taken from Canadian waters, and there are probably as many 5-pound-plus smallmouth caught in the North as in the South.

How to Select Lures Based on Stomach Contents

WHOLE CRAYFISH or crayfish parts mean a crayfish-colored crankbait may be effective.

SHINER MINNOWS mean that a small, silver-colored minnow plug would be a good choice.

IMMATURE INSECTS can be imitated with a dark-colored jig or a nymph.

ADULT INSECTS indicate that smallmouth will probably take a large dry fly or a bass bug.

Growth Rates of Smallmouth Bass at Different Latitudes

Lake Name and Latitude	Length in Inches at Various Ages									
	Age 1	2	3	4	5	6	7	8	9	10
Lake Opeongo, Ont. (46°N)	2.1	5.2	7.7	9.1	11.1	12.2	13.5	14.5	15.5	—
Northern Lake Michigan (45°N)	3.9	6.3	8.1	9.7	11.5	13.2	14.6	15.8	16.8	17.4
Lake Simcoe, Ont. (44°N)	4.2	6.3	8.6	10.9	13.0	14.6	15.8	16.9	17.0	—
Quabbin Lake, Mass. (42½°N)	3.5	6.7	10.2	12.9	14.7	16.1	16.7	17.1	17.3	17.5
Pine Flat Lake, Cal. (37°N)	5.5	8.9	12.5	14.7	16.6	17.9	18.3	—	—	—
Norris Lake, Tenn. (36°N)	3.1	8.9	13.3	15.8	17.4	18.0	18.6	20.9	—	—
Pickwick Lake, Ala. (35°N)	5.9	10.7	13.5	16.6	18.5	20.4	21.0	21.6	—	—

HIGH-COMPETITION situations cause smallmouth bass to be extremely aggressive. They are not linked tightly to cover and do not hesitate to chase their prey into open water. When you hook a smallmouth and reel it in, it is not unusual to see a dozen more following in an attempt to steal the bait from the hooked fish. Or, you may see a smallmouth swirl at your lure just as you lift it from the water.

Competition

Experienced smallmouth fishermen know that smallmouth behave much differently in different bodies of water, so they alter their fishing strategy to suit the situation. To a large extent, these differences in behavior depend on the level of competition among the smallmouth population.

In a body of water where smallmouth are scarce and food is abundant, the level of competition generally is low. But if smallmouth are numerous and food is hard to find, the competition level is likely to be high. Smallmouth are much more aggressive, less cautious, and considerably easier to catch in a high-competition environment.

The level of competition can make a big difference not only in your fishing strategy, but also in your choice of fishing waters.

Competition can affect your choice of lures and baits and your method of presentation. A fast-moving crankbait, for example, is more likely to trigger strikes in high-competition waters. Smallmouth in these waters are conditioned to chase their food. The fish that gets to the minnow first may be the only one that eats.

In low-competition waters, crankbaits and other fast-moving lures have less appeal. Smallmouth ex-

amine their food more closely, so a slow live-bait presentation will usually draw more strikes.

If you must fish after a cold front or under other adverse weather conditions, choose a body of water where the competition level is high. When food is scarce, smallmouth must continue to feed despite changing weather.

The level of competition can also determine the time of day when fishing is best. In low-competition waters, smallmouth normally feed most heavily in early morning and late afternoon, when light levels are relatively low. But in high-competition waters, they usually feed all day.

Although ice fishing for smallmouth is usually a waste of time in low-competition waters, smallmouth sometimes bite all winter long in high-competition waters.

The level of competition in a given body of water can vary from year to year as the smallmouth population and the food crop fluctuate in size. These fluctuations are the major reasons that fishing can be good one year and poor the next.

It may be difficult for a fisherman to gauge the level of competition in a body of water, but the indicators shown below will help.

Indicators of the Level of Competition

HEAVY FISHING PRESSURE is likely to reduce the smallmouth population enough to keep the level of competition low.

GOOD HABITAT, such as a cool, clear lake with a rocky shoreline, usually means smallmouth are abundant and the competition level high.

PREDATORS that occupy shallow water, like northerns and largemouth, compete with smallmouth. If they are numerous, competition is high.

How Weather Affects Smallmouth

Weather plays a major role in smallmouth fishing. If you had a choice of when to fish, your odds would undoubtedly be best during a period of stable weather. Changes in the weather disrupt the smallmouth's feeding schedule. They may continue to feed, but peak feeding times are not as predictable. Exactly how changes in weather affect smallmouth depends on time of year, type of water, and even type of cover. Following are the weather conditions that have the most influence on smallmouth fishing:

CLOUD COVER. Smallmouth normally bite better when the skies are overcast rather than clear. Although smallmouth are not as light-sensitive as walleyes, low light causes them to move into shallow water and feed more heavily.

But clear weather is nearly always better in early spring, because the sun warms the water and urges smallmouth to begin feeding.

The degree to which cloud cover affects smallmouth fishing depends on the clarity of the water. In lakes that are extremely clear, daytime fishing is usually poor when skies are sunny. In these waters, smallmouth do much of their feeding at night. But in lakes of moderate clarity, they feed sporadically throughout the day even though the skies are clear.

WIND. Windy weather generally spells good smallmouth fishing. The waves scatter the light rays so less light penetrates the surface and smallmouth feeding increases.

In a shallow body of water, a strong wind stirs up the bottom, making the water so murky that smallmouth cannot see well enough to feed. Fishing remains slow until the water starts to clear.

Windy weather may also cause poor fishing when smallmouth are in the weeds. The movement of the vegetation caused by the wave action seems to make them extra-cautious.

RAIN. Rainy weather usually improves smallmouth fishing, especially when the surface is calm. Overcast skies combined with rain droplets dimpling the surface decrease the amount of light that penetrates. And the sound seems to reduce the chance of spooking the fish.

Rain has practically no effect on fishing on a windy day. Because light penetration is already low and the level of background sound is high, smallmouth are not as spooky as in calm weather.

A warm rain in early spring can make a big difference in fishing success. The water temperature may rise several degrees in one day, resulting in an insect hatch which causes semi-dormant smallmouth to start feeding.

A heavy rain usually means poor fishing in streams. Runoff clouds the water so smallmouth cannot see your bait as well. And rising water spreads the fish over a larger area, so finding them is more difficult.

Storms accompanied by lightning and loud thunderclaps cause smallmouth to stop biting. Fishing stays slow for several days if the storm is severe.

COLD FRONTS. Smallmouth often go on a feeding spree before a storm, but if the temperature drops dramatically and the skies clear following the storm, catching them becomes tough.

The negative effects of a cold front are most noticeable in spring and summer, especially if the front follows a period of warm, stable weather. Smallmouth feed heavily during the warm weather, so they can afford to stop for a few days after the cold front passes.

Cold fronts usually do not slow feeding in fall. In fact, it seems as if smallmouth sense the approach of winter and begin feeding more heavily. Anglers willing to brave the elements can enjoy some of the year's best fishing.

The effects of a cold front on smallmouth, as on many other freshwater gamefish, are more severe in clear lakes than in murkier lakes or in rivers.

BAROMETRIC PRESSURE. Most experienced smallmouth fishermen believe that barometric pressure has little effect on fishing success.

ROUGH WATER scatters the light rays that strike the surface, causing much less light to penetrate than if the surface were calm. The lower light level causes smallmouth to move shallower and feed.

CROSSWINDS blowing over the underwater extension of a point or over a reef wash plankton and insect larvae loose from the bottom and carry them to the downwind side. The drifting food attracts baitfish and smallmouth.

ONSHORE WINDS wash plankton in to shore and churn up the water, causing a *mudline*. Baitfish move in to feed on the plankton and the light level is low enough for smallmouth to feed in the shallows.

WIND-INDUCED CURRENTS draw smallmouth into narrows and into troughs between islands or between an island and the lakeshore. The current attracts baitfish and the narrows or trough concentrates them.

34

How Moon Phase
Affects Smallmouth Fishing

Many smallmouth-fishing authorities prefer to fish on the days around the full moon, particularly the days just before it. They maintain that night fishing is better around the full moon, although daytime fishing may be slower, especially in clear lakes.

Summertime anglers on southern reservoirs do most of their smallmouth fishing at night, during the full moon. Some maintain that smallmouth bite better in the full moon, but others say that the biggest reason for fishing at that time is to see where they are going.

Most fisheries biologists and angling experts discount the importance of moon phase. They consider time of day and the weather much more important.

To evaluate the effects of moon phase on smallmouth fishing, Hunting & Fishing Library researchers contacted conservation agencies throughout the country. They compiled records of the biggest smallmouth and the dates when they were caught, then correlated those dates with the moon phase. No information is available on what time of day the fish were caught, but most were probably taken in daylight hours. The results are shown below.

	Percentage of Big Smallmouth Caught in Each Moon Phase by Region				Total Percentage Caught in United States
MOON PHASES	EASTERN STATES	SOUTH-CENTRAL STATES	NORTH-CENTRAL STATES	WESTERN STATES	TOTAL
New	25%	21%	27%	23%	**24%**
First Quarter	26%	34%	36%	32%	**30%**
Full	25%	34%	24%	18%	**26%**
Last Quarter	24%	11%	13%	27%	**20%**

FISHING SUCCESS, as indicated by a sample of more than 200 big smallmouth caught around the country, is generally best during the first-quarter and full moon, and poorest around the last-quarter moon. In the south-central states, for instance, anglers caught about three times as many fish during the first-quarter and full moon as in the last quarter. Figures for each phase include data from 3 days on either side, for a total of 7 days.

Spawning Behavior

Smallmouth bass can spawn successfully in lakes or streams, and the areas they choose for spawning in streams differ very little from the areas they choose in lakes.

A typical spawning site is near an object like a rock or log which shelters it from strong current or wave action. Such an object also makes it easier for a male to guard the nest because predators cannot sneak in from behind. Nests are usually in water 2 to 4 feet deep, although they have been found in water as deep as 20 feet. Smallmouth almost always nest on sand, gravel or rubble and avoid mud bottoms.

Males begin building nests in spring, when the water temperature stabilizes above 55°F. The male uses his tail to fan out a circular nest with a diameter about twice as great as his own length. On a rubble bottom, he simply sweeps debris off the rocks. But on a sand or gravel bottom, he fans out a depression from 2 to 4 inches deep. A male nests in the same general area each year and will sometimes use the same nest.

Females move into the vicinity of the nest a few days later. When a male spots a female, he rushes toward her and attempts to drive her to the nest. At first, she swims away, but she returns again later. Eventually, the male coaxes her to the nest. Spawning usually occurs at a water temperature of 60° to 65°F, about 3 degrees cooler than the typical spawning temperature of largemouth bass.

As the spawning act begins, the fish lie side by side, both facing the same direction. Then the female tips on her side to deposit her eggs and the male simultaneously releases his milt. Females deposit an average of 7,000 eggs per pound of body weight.

The female leaves after spawning, but the male remains and vigorously guards the nest against any intruders. He will attack fish much larger than himself and may even bump a wading fisherman who gets too close. The amount of time required for hatching depends on water temperature. At 54°F, the eggs hatch in ten days; at 77°, two days. On the average, 35 percent of the eggs hatch.

The male guards the fry on the nest for 5 to 7 days and usually continues to guard them for another week or two after the school leaves the nest. Of the fry that leave the nest, only about 10 percent survive to fingerling size.

Fishermen can destroy smallmouth nests by stepping on them or by catching the guarding male. If panfish are numerous, they quickly consume the eggs or fry once the male is gone.

SHOWN 6 TIMES ACTUAL SIZE

FRY are transparent when first hatched. They have a large, yellowish egg sac that nurtures them through the first 6 to 12 days of life.

SHOWN TWICE ACTUAL SIZE

BLACK COLORATION begins to appear within a few days after the fry hatch. This explains the origin of the term *black bass*.

SHOWN ONE-THIRD ACTUAL SIZE

FINGERLINGS are 3 to 5 inches long by the end of the first summer. The tail fin has a brownish-orange base and a distinct whitish margin.

MALES guard the fry (small black spots in foreground) to protect them against predators, particularly small panfish. In one study, a single bluegill ate 39 smallmouth fry when the male was momentarily driven away.

Homing

The homing tendency of smallmouth bass is among the strongest of all freshwater gamefish. In a lake or reservoir, a smallmouth may spend most of its time along a stretch of shoreline only a hundred yards long. In a stream, a smallmouth may stay in one pool that fulfills all its needs for food and cover.

Smallmouth may leave these home areas to find good spawning habitat or a deep wintering area, but during the rest of the year they stray very little.

Each spring, smallmouth return to the same area to spawn. Even high water does not discourage them from returning to their traditional spawning sites. So once you find a spawning concentration, you can bet the smallmouth will be there again the next year.

Even the wintering areas remain the same from year to year. In late fall, when the water temperature drops below 50°F, fishermen familiar with the water know exactly which sharp-dropping points and steep breaks will hold the smallmouth.

Immature smallmouth tend to wander more than the adults. One possible explanation is that the larger, more assertive smallmouth take over the best feeding and resting areas. The smaller fish are forced to move about to find suitable habitat.

The study depicted on these pages was conducted on a typical midwestern smallmouth stream. It shows the strong homing tendency of stream-dwelling smallmouth. The smallmouth were captured, tagged, transferred to a different area of the stream, then released. In most cases, the transferred smallmouth found their way back to the pool in which they were captured, passing through several other pools along the way that offered suitable habitat. Some of them were transferred two or three times, and found their way back each time.

Homing Behavior of Smallmouth Bass in a Midwestern Stream
(photos simulate an actual study conducted in Jordan Creek, Illinois)

TAGGING. Smallmouth captured in their home pool (Pool A on map at upper right) were measured, then numbered tags were attached for identification.

TRANSFERRING. Tagged fish were placed in an aerated tank so they could be transferred from their home pool to another pool on the same stream.

Study Section — Jordan Creek, Illinois

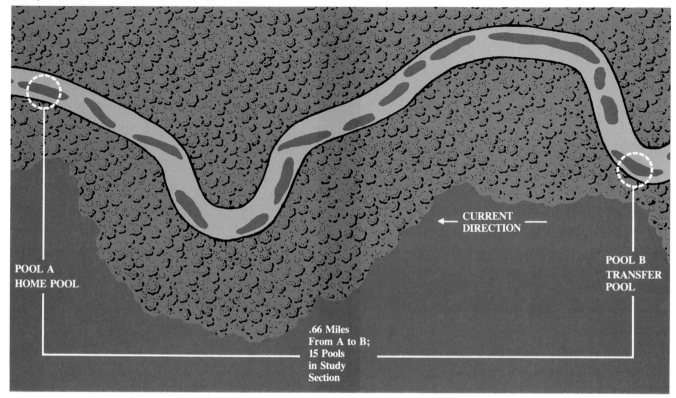

CURRENT DIRECTION

POOL A
HOME POOL

POOL B
TRANSFER
POOL

.66 Miles
From A to B;
15 Pools
in Study
Section

RELEASING. The tagged smallmouth were released into Pool B, about two-thirds of a mile upstream. Over the summer, a total of 13 releases were made.

RECAPTURING. In 9 of 13 cases, the tagged smallmouth released into Pool B were later recaptured in Pool A. To reach Pool A, they bypassed 13 other pools.

Where to Find Smallmouth

BRAGGING BOARDS found in many bait shops and tackle stores can give you some valuable clues on locating good smallmouth water. Although the photos may be dark and out of focus, they usually list the name of the lake or river where the fish was caught. In some instances, they also reveal the date the fish was caught and the bait or lure used to catch it. Pay most attention to photos of smallmouth taken in the last year or two.

How to Select Smallmouth Waters

Finding a lake or stream with a good smallmouth population can be difficult. Because smallmouth prefer the cleanest and clearest waters available, they generally inhabit a smaller percentage of the waters in a given region than most other gamefish do. And because smallmouth are fairly easy to catch, a healthy population can be fished down quickly once the word gets out.

Natural-resources agencies may not be able to give you much help because smallmouth are difficult to sample. A lake or stream may have lots of smallmouth, but few are found in fish-population surveys because they are very net-shy. They avoid gill nets, trap nets and most other sampling gear, but can be sampled by shocking. Results of shocking surveys are available from some natural-resources agencies.

You can sometimes get good information from tackle shops, marinas and knowledgeable fishermen who have firsthand experience on waters in the area where you will be fishing. You can also find good smallmouth waters by paying attention to fishing-contest results, newspaper reports, regional magazine articles and local outdoor programs on radio and television. If a lake or river is consistently producing smallmouth, chances are you will find out about it through these sources.

The surest way to find a good lake or stream is to hire a competent guide who specializes in smallmouth. He will take you to his prime waters and best spots. And once you get to know him, he may be willing to share his knowledge of other good smallmouth waters.

How Survey Data Can Help You Find Good Smallmouth Water

SHOCKING is an effective way for natural-resources agencies to sample smallmouth populations in streams. Current from the electrodes temporarily stuns the fish so they can be weighed and measured.

SURVEY REPORTS list shocking results, including the number of fish per hour of shocking or per acre of water. This report shows that the smallmouth population is highest in sectors 3 to 6.

SURFACE ACTIVITY of baitfish can help you recognize structure that holds smallmouth. If the structure holds a lot of baitfish, you can often see them feeding on the surface in early morning or at dusk. In some cases, largemouth or white bass can be seen taking baitfish on the surface while smallmouth feed below.

How to Recognize Smallmouth Structure

Smallmouth are like most other warmwater gamefish in that structure, which is the topography of the lake or stream bed, dictates where they are found.

A piece of structure that provides food, cover and easy access to the depths may hold smallmouth through the entire year. They simply move deeper or shallower as the seasons change. But if the structure lacks one of these vital elements, smallmouth will move to different pieces of structure to find what they need.

If you find smallmouth spawning in 3 feet of water on a sand-gravel point, you may find them on the same point in summer, but in 12 to 18 feet of water, especially if there are boulders or weeds for cover. In late fall, they will probably stay on the same point but drop into 30 to 50 feet of water.

But if the point lacks summertime cover, smallmouth cannot escape the sunlight, so they will move to structure that offers shade. If the point flattens out at 25 feet, smallmouth may stay there through summer, but will move to a deeper point or offshore reef in late fall.

A good flasher is a must in checking potential smallmouth structure. Smallmouth are almost always found over a hard bottom. By carefully watching for a strong signal, you can quickly locate hard-bottomed areas at the likely depth range.

To understand how a flasher can save fishing time, consider this example. After examining your lake map, you conclude there is a good chance of finding smallmouth along an irregular sandy breakline that runs the length of the north shore. You could try trolling the breakline to find the smallmouth, but that would take several hours. Instead, run the breakline at full speed and watch your flasher for a particularly strong signal which indicates an area of rock or gravel. In only a few minutes, you can pinpoint likely smallmouth spots.

Resort owners or marinas and dock operators may be able to identify specific points, humps or other spots that have been consistently producing smallmouth. If you have a lake map, ask them to mark the spots for you. If you are lucky enough to find a local fishing expert who is willing to share some of his secrets, be careful about the questions you ask. Few serious fishermen are willing to reveal their prime spots, but they will usually tell you what type of structure to look for, and the best depths to fish.

Above-water indicators reveal a great deal about smallmouth structure, if you know what to look for. The examples on the opposite page show how to interpret these clues.

The exact type of structure that smallmouth occupy in different seasons varies greatly, depending on the type of water. For suggestions on where to look for smallmouth in the waters you fish, check the examples on pages 50 to 69.

CHANGES in soil composition along the shoreline usually reveal similar changes below water. If you see a line where the soil changes abruptly from sand to rock, visually extend the line into the water. Smallmouth often congregate along the rock margin.

AQUATIC VEGETATION along the shoreline can also provide clues to bottom type. If cattails grow along shore, the bottom probably consists of mud. But bulrushes usually mean a bottom of hard sand or rock, materials better suited to smallmouth.

DEGREE OF SLOPE of the underwater portion of a point can usually be determined by the slope of the above-water portion. A gradually sloping point is normally the best choice in spring; a point with a steeper slope in summer and fall.

JAGGED BLUFFS with many lips and crevices above the water line indicate good smallmouth habitat below water. These irregularities provide shade and attract smallmouth foods. A smooth bluff face lacks these nooks and crannies and holds fewer smallmouth.

How to Recognize
Good Smallmouth Cover

Finding productive smallmouth water and determining the type of structure most likely to hold smallmouth are vital to consistent fishing success. But there is still one more piece to the puzzle: you must be able to recognize the specific types of cover that smallmouth prefer.

The primary component of good smallmouth cover is shade, but smallmouth will not use the cover unless a good food supply and deep water are within easy reach. The best cover offers overhead protection as well as shade.

Let's assume that you have located a reef that looks perfect for smallmouth. It is surrounded by deep water and consists mostly of marble- to golfball-sized rock, with a section of scattered boulders along one edge. The entire reef has a good supply of smallmouth foods like crayfish, insect larvae and baitfish, but only the section with the boulders offers adequate shade. This section will hold many more smallmouth than other parts of the reef.

The type of cover that smallmouth use is greatly influenced by other shallow-water predators. If a body of water has a high population of largemouth bass or northern pike, they will occupy weedbeds and woody cover, forcing smallmouth to seek other cover options. But if there are few largemouth or northerns, the weedbeds and woody cover will probably draw smallmouth.

Good Rocks vs. Bad Rocks

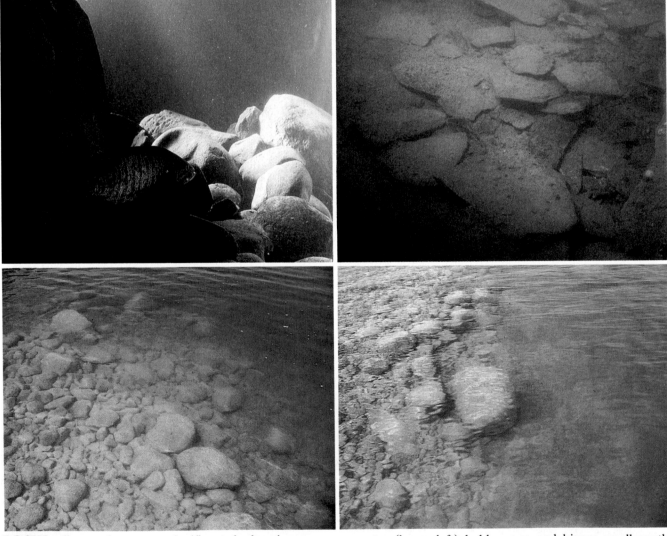

ROCKS tall enough to cast a significant shadow (upper left) make better smallmouth cover than flat rocks (upper right). A reef with large rocks continuing well into deep water (lower left) holds more and bigger smallmouth than a reef that has rocks on the top but sand or silt sloping into deep water (lower right).

Good Stumps vs. Bad Stumps

STUMPS with openings between washed-out roots (left) offer overhead cover in addition to shade. This type of stump is much more likely to hold smallmouth than one with embedded roots (right).

Good Trees vs. Bad Trees

FALLEN TREES that have thick trunks and limbs and slope sharply into the water (left) are best for smallmouth. The thick trunk and limbs offer shade and overhead cover, and the steep slope shows that there is deep water nearby. Spindly trees (right) seldom hold smallmouth, but are attractive to largemouth.

Good Weeds vs. Bad Weeds

WEEDS that grow on a firm sand-gravel bottom, such as wild celery (left) and bulrushes, are more attractive to smallmouth than weeds that grow on a soft bottom, like lily pads (right) and cattails. Hard-bottom plants located along a breakline attract more smallmouth than those on a shallow flat with no deep water nearby.

Where to Find Smallmouth Through the Seasons

Although smallmouth are less migratory than most other freshwater gamefish, you must be familiar with their seasonal movement patterns for consistent fishing success. In many waters, smallmouth stay in the same vicinity all year. The secret to finding them in different seasons may simply be to fish shallower or deeper.

Regardless of the type of water, smallmouth seasonal movements are controlled by the same factors and are surprisingly predictable.

SPRING. Smallmouth remain in a state of near-dormancy until the water temperature approaches 50°F. Then they begin moving toward their spawning areas. In streams, the spawning migration may begin at lower temperatures. The exact sites chosen for spawning depend on the type of water. Because smallmouth have a strong homing instinct, they normally spawn in the same area each year.

After recuperating from spawning, the females scatter to deeper water. Males move deeper once they abandon the fry. Both sexes remain in the vicinity of their spawning sites, if there is deep water nearby. Although they are feeding more heavily now than during the spawning period, fishing may be tough because they are not as concentrated.

SUMMER. Smallmouth are even more predictable in summer than during other seasons. Once they take up residence on a particular piece of structure or in a certain pool, they may not move for several months. This stay-at-home tendency can be partially explained by the smallmouth's strong liking for crayfish. Unlike most other types of smallmouth food, crayfish are linked to a specific location. They require rocks for protection and cannot move far from cover. But in waters where baitfish are the primary food, smallmouth must move around to find them.

Deep water is particularly important in summer. With the surface temperature high and the sun directly overhead, smallmouth must retreat to deep water to find a comfortable temperature and light level. How deep they go varies with the type of water. In a clear lake, they may go as deep as 25 feet.

In a murky lake that lacks oxygen in the depths, they may be restricted to water shallower than 12 feet. In a small stream, they may spend the summer in pools only 4 feet deep because there is no deeper water.

EARLY TO MID-FALL. Early fall finds smallmouth in much the same locations as they were in summer, although they spend more of their time in shallow water. The shallows offer more food, and because of the cooler surface temperatures and lower sun angle, smallmouth have no need to go deep.

In most lakes, the surface continues to cool and eventually reaches the same temperature as the water below the thermocline. When this happens, the lake turns over, meaning that all of the water circulates and the temperature becomes the same from top to bottom. You may catch one smallmouth at a depth of 5 feet and another at 30 feet. The lack of a consistent pattern results in tough fishing.

In rivers, smallmouth remain in their early-fall locations through mid-fall. They feed more as the water cools, so mid-fall fishing can be the best of the year, particularly for good-sized smallmouth.

LATE FALL AND WINTER. Following the turnover, the likelihood of finding smallmouth in the shallows diminishes. However, a few days of warm weather may draw baitfish into shallow water and attract smallmouth.

Once smallmouth retreat to deep water, they feed very little. Many fishermen believe that smallmouth simply cannot be caught under these conditions, but if you take the time to do some thorough scouting, you can sometimes locate small but densely packed schools. Although smallmouth are not actively feeding, a slow presentation will tempt a few bites. And the fish you catch are likely to be big.

Stream smallmouth may move to deep pools if their mid-fall locations are too shallow for wintering. They continue to feed and fishing is good until the water temperature drops into the low 40s.

To get a better idea of the seasonal movements of smallmouth bass in the specific types of water you fish, refer to pages 50 to 69.

Mesotrophic Lakes

These moderately fertile lakes rank among the top producers of smallmouth bass. The meso lakes best suited to smallmouth have clean, well-structured bottoms; enough sand-gravel or rock areas to provide spawning habitat and produce crayfish; and low populations of competitor species, especially largemouth bass and northern pike.

Several weeks before spawning, when the water temperature reaches the mid-40s, smallmouth in meso lakes begin moving from their deep wintering areas toward the areas where they will spawn. On calm, sunny days, they swim into the shallows to feed on minnows and insects. Dark-bottomed bays and shallow flats with lots of exposed boulders warm most quickly and are the first to attract small-mouth, especially if these areas are near the spawning grounds.

Periodic cold fronts during the pre-spawn period will drive most smallmouth to deeper water, usually back to the breakline. But the females stop making these in-and-out movements once their eggs near ripeness. They stay in deep water until the time comes to spawn.

Males build the nests in 2 to 8 feet of water, usually in bays or along shorelines protected from the wind. The nests are generally next to boulders, logs, boat-mooring blocks, or any other solid object in the water. Smallmouth will also spawn in emergent vegetation, especially bulrushes, if largemouth are not using it.

Other spawning areas include rocky main-lake points and submerged humps. But water in the main lake takes longer to warm, so spawning takes place a week or two later than spawning in bays or along sheltered shorelines.

After spawning, females return to deep water where they spend at least two weeks regaining their

strength. They refuse to bite during this time. Males stay with the fry for up to three weeks.

When the recuperation and fry-guarding period is over, smallmouth begin feeding heavily. They may be found just about anywhere. Some roam the shoreline in search of small baitfish, others work muddy flats to find emerging insects, and still others move to rocky offshore structure where they can feed on crayfish. Because they seldom stay in one place for long, finding them may be difficult.

Smallmouth gradually move to deeper water, and by the time the water temperature reaches 65° to 70°F, they have reached the locations where they will spend the summer. Although summertime structure is quite varied, it usually falls in a depth range of 10 to 20 feet.

The main ingredients of summertime smallmouth habitat are a good food supply, adequate cover, and easy access to deep water. The right type of bottom is also important. In most meso lakes, smallmouth prefer rock, gravel or a combination of the two. But if the basin consists mostly of rock or gravel, small-

mouth are often found on sandy, weedy bottoms. Sandy areas are also a good choice in lakes where most of the bottom is muddy.

Smallmouth remain in their summertime haunts through early fall. But as the surface cools, they move into the shallows where they feed heavily until the turnover. They scatter while the turnover is in progress. When the surface water cools to the upper 40s, they move much deeper, usually to depths of 25 to 40 feet and sometimes to depths of 50 feet or more. Prime late-fall areas are in deep water just off summertime structure that borders large, open areas of the lake. Smallmouth tend to hold at the base of the drop-offs.

Although smallmouth become much less active in late fall, a period of warm, calm weather may draw them into shallower water and trigger some feeding. But when the water temperature drops below 40°F, they form extremely tight schools and become semi-dormant. A storm in late fall may spur some deep-water feeding. Only in high-competition lakes (pages 30-31) will smallmouth feed regularly in late fall and winter.

Seasonal Location in Mesotrophic Lakes

SAND-GRAVEL BAYS protected from the wind are prime spawning areas. Some deep bays may hold smallmouth until fall.

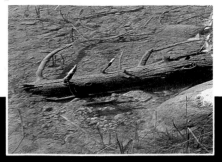

WOODY DEBRIS over a firm sand or gravel bottom provides smallmouth with excellent nesting cover.

BULRUSH BEDS adjacent to deep water are good spawning areas. They also serve as feeding areas through summer.

DOCKS, fallen trees and other shallow-water cover near spawning areas concentrate pre-spawn smallmouth.

DARK-BOTTOMED BAYS warm fastest, so they offer the earliest source of food for pre-spawn smallmouth.

GRADUALLY SLOPING POINTS are good spawning areas. Before and after spawn-ing, smallmouth hold along the drop-off.

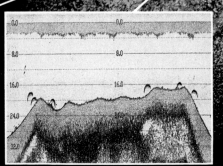

DEEP HUMPS near summertime small-mouth habitat attract smallmouth in late fall and into the winter.

IRREGULAR BREAKLINES that plunge sharply into deep water are good late-fall smallmouth spots.

MODERATELY SLOPING POINTS draw smallmouth after spawning and continue to hold them into early fall.

FLATS near deep water are major feeding areas from early spring into early fall. Good flats have cover like rocks or logs.

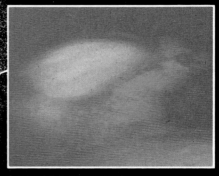

SAND-GRAVEL HUMPS, especially those with sparse weed growth, rank among the top summertime smallmouth spots.

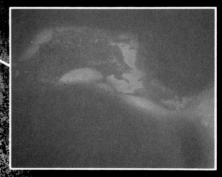

CABBAGE BEDS adjoining deep water make ideal spots for smallmouth to ambush food, particularly in summer.

STEEP-SLOPING POINTS concentrate smallmouth in late fall and continue to hold them into the winter.

SANDGRASS growing along a moderate drop-off is likely to hold smallmouth from early summer to early fall.

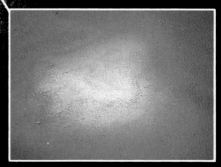

ROCKY REEFS, particularly those with a scattering of large boulders, hold smallmouth in summer and early fall.

Oligotrophic Lakes

The cold, infertile waters of most oligotrophic lakes are best suited to lake trout, northern pike and walleyes. But many of these lakes have warm, shallow sections that more closely resemble mesotrophic lakes. These sections often hold tremendous numbers of smallmouth bass.

The key to finding smallmouth in oligotrophic lakes is learning to identify these prime areas. Because most oligotrophic lakes have an abundance of rocky habitat that looks good for smallmouth, the best areas may not be easy to recognize.

Depth is the major consideration. If half of a lake averages 100 feet deep and the other half 30 feet deep, you can bet that the vast majority of smallmouth will be found in the 30-foot portion, where the water is warmer and food more abundant. If you do not have a contour map of the lake, the easiest way to identify smallmouth water is to look for clusters of islands, preferably islands surrounded by large shoal areas.

Smallmouth may winter in the deeper portions of oligotrophic lakes, especially if the shallow portions lack deep holding areas. But when the water temperature rises to the mid-40s in spring, smallmouth begin moving toward the shallower areas.

Areas that seem suitable for spawning are almost everywhere, but the sites actually chosen are in the areas that warm earliest. Protected bays or shoals around island clusters are excellent spawning areas.

Prior to spawning, smallmouth hold along the first major drop-off out from the spawning area, provided that the drop-off leads into water at least 15 feet deep. A period of calm, sunny weather warms the water enough to draw smallmouth into the shallows, but they move out again when the water cools. When the water temperature reaches the mid-50s, males stay in the shallows and begin to fan out nests.

The nests are usually in 2 to 6 feet of water next to a boulder, especially one that is partially exposed rather than completely submerged. Exposed boulders will absorb more heat from the sun, so they warm more quickly and in turn warm the water around them.

Because the water generally warms more slowly in oligotrophic lakes than in other types of waters, smallmouth may spawn at temperatures cooler than normal. It is not unusual for spawning to start at

55°F. The spawning period lasts from 6 to 10 days, although not all smallmouth spawn at once. A sudden cold snap, a common occurrence on oligotrophic lakes, may cause smallmouth to abort their spawning activity and leave the nests. If spawning activity is aborted several times, females may resorb their eggs.

The slower warming of these lakes also means that the females need extra time to recuperate from spawning. And the fry develop more slowly, so the males spend more time guarding them. The recuperating and guarding periods last about a week longer than in a typical meso lake.

Both males and females then scatter in search of food. Some can be found in shallow, mucky bays while others feed in deep water. Finding a consistent pattern is difficult at this time. To further complicate matters, some males may still be guarding their fry and some females still recuperating.

Smallmouth may not have to move far from their spawning areas to find summertime habitat. Most oligotrophic lakes that hold smallmouth are in the northern states or southern Canada where surface temperatures seldom rise above the low 70s. Many of these lakes have a light to moderate bog stain, so sunlight does not penetrate as deep as in clear mesotrophic lakes. As a result, smallmouth seldom need to move to deep water.

The best summertime smallmouth habitat generally has a bottom of baseball- to basketball-sized rock. This type of bottom has plenty of hiding places for crayfish, insect larvae and other invertebrates. It also offers good cover. Smallmouth are rarely found over a bottom of large slab rock. Typical summertime depths range from 8 to 15 feet. Easy access to deep water is less important in oligotrophic lakes than in mesotrophic lakes.

As in meso lakes, smallmouth may prefer sandy, weedy bottoms, especially if the rest of the basin consists primarily of rock. The weedy habitat attracts more baitfish. It is not unusual to find summertime smallmouth in sandy bays or over sandy offshore humps.

Smallmouth stay near their summertime habitat until the fall turnover. They may remain there after the turnover, if the structure drops rapidly into 30 to 50 feet of water. If not, they move to deep reefs or rocky points that slope sharply into the depths.

Although smallmouth continue to feed through late fall, finding them can be difficult. They form very tight schools, usually next to rock piles or deep weed beds. Or, a school may tuck into a sharp inside turn along the breakline. Once the water temperature drops below 40°F, smallmouth become nearly dormant. But in high-competition lakes (pages 30-31), they may continue to feed through the winter.

Seasonal Location in Oligotrophic Lakes

DROP-OFFS adjacent to spawning sites are the primary staging areas for pre-spawn smallmouth bass.

SHALLOW, SANDY BAYS warm earlier than the main lake and make excellent spawning areas for smallmouth.

POINTS at the mouths of spawning bays hold post-spawn smallmouth until they are ready to move into the main lake.

SMALL CREEKS draining bog areas warm early. Smallmouth congregate around the mouth prior to spawning.

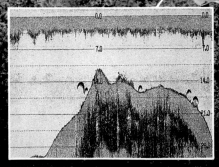

DEEP REEFS in shallower portions of the main lake hold smallmouth from late fall into the winter.

BREAKLINES where shoreline flats plunge into deep water are likely to draw smallmouth in late fall and winter.

ISLAND CLUSTERS with a lot of shoal area provide good spawning habitat and usually hold smallmouth through summer.

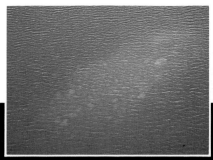

SHALLOW, ROCKY REEFS close to shore draw smallmouth after spawning and continue to hold them through summer.

MOUTHS of major inlets offer current, food, and warmer water. They attract smallmouth from late spring through summer.

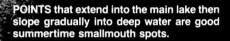

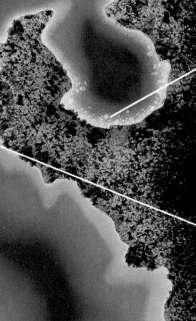

POINTS that extend into the main lake then slope gradually into deep water are good summertime smallmouth spots.

SANDY BAYS with moderately deep water and some weeds hold good numbers of smallmouth in summer and early fall.

POINTS that extend into the main lake then drop sharply into deep water are the best late-fall and winter spots.

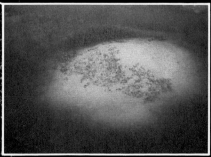

SANDY HUMPS with scattered weeds are also good in summer and early fall, especially if the basin is primarily rock.

Eutrophic Lakes

These fertile lakes are shallow, warm and weedy. They have silty bottoms and often lack well-defined structure. Eutrophic lakes are best suited to large-mouth, but some hold a few smallmouth, often fish of trophy size.

Because of the silty bottom, spawning sites are scarce. Smallmouth will spawn on rocky points or along sand-gravel or rock shorelines in protected bays, usually at depths of 4 feet or less. If there is no rock or gravel, smallmouth may be able to fan away the silt to reach a firm bottom.

Before spawning, smallmouth cruise the breakline in the vicinity of the nesting area. You can generally find them at depths of 5 to 10 feet. After spawning

has been completed, they begin scattering to their summer locations.

In lakes with some structure, smallmouth spend the summer on points that drop into the deepest water, along inside turns on the breakline, and around offshore humps. In bowl-shaped lakes, they relate to the outside edge of the weedline.

As summer progresses, rising water temperatures drive the smallmouth to deeper water. However, most eutrophic lakes do not have adequate oxygen below the thermocline during the summer months, so smallmouth must stay at depths of 15 feet or less.

Smallmouth remain in their summertime locations until the submerged weeds begin to die off in fall. By late fall, you can find them at the base of points and humps, usually at depths of 20 to 30 feet. In structureless lakes, hard-bottomed areas that rise only a foot above the rest of the bottom may draw small-mouth. They remain in these locations through winter, but do not feed regularly.

Pits

Pits created by various types of mining operations provide good smallmouth habitat once mining is discontinued and the pits fill with water. Gravel pits and rock quarries are the most common types of smallmouth pit. But other types, like coal and iron ore pits, may hold some smallmouth.

The best smallmouth pits have banks with moderate slopes and ample cover in the form of rock slides, submerged trees, and ledges along old roads used to haul out gravel, rock or coal.

Some pits have extremely steep banks and drop quickly to depths of 100 feet or more. Because the sheer banks offer no spawning habitat and little cover, these pits hold few smallmouth.

It is difficult to generalize about the seasonal movements of smallmouth bass in pits because of the great differences in structure. In the gravel pit shown in the above photo, most smallmouth would spend the entire year in the portion of the pit with the roadbed. A few fish may relate to fallen trees and crevices along the steep banks, but most prefer the stair-step ledges along the road.

In pits with moderately sloping banks and a variety of structure, smallmouth behave much the same as in a mesotrophic lake (pages 50 to 53). In pits with gradually sloping banks and little structure, they are found in the same types of habitat as in a shallow, eutrophic lake (opposite page). In deep pits with sheer, cliff-like walls, smallmouth behave more as they would in a canyon reservoir (page 65).

Many pits are located on privately owned land and do not have a public access. But if you take the time to ask, landowners will often give you permission to fish and may even give you some tips on where to find the smallmouth.

Mid-Depth Reservoirs

Mid-depth reservoirs produce more big smallmouth than any other type of water. They have an abundance of shallow rock and gravel spawning areas, plenty of hard-bottomed structure adjacent to deep water, and a good supply of smallmouth foods like crayfish and shad. The large reservoirs in mid-South states like Kentucky and Tennessee are the best producers of big smallmouth. They have a much longer growing season than reservoirs in the North.

Smallmouth generally spend the winter in deep water off shoreline points or steep-sloping banks, or in deep areas of the old river channel. As the water starts to warm in spring, they begin moving toward their spawning areas.

Shallow creek arms warm earlier than other areas of the reservoir and are the first to attract pre-spawn smallmouth. Shallow points in the main reservoir and eddies in the tailrace also attract them. Because the upper end of a reservoir warms earlier than the lower end, pre-spawn movements take place sooner on the upper end.

Most mid-depth reservoirs are fairly clear, so smallmouth build their nests in deep water, usually 3 to 10 feet, but sometimes as deep as 15 feet. Nests are usually on gradually sloping bottoms of rock or gravel mixed with clay. As in other types of waters, smallmouth nest near boulders, logs or stumps.

At the upper end of a large reservoir, smallmouth may complete spawning a month earlier than at the lower end. As a result, smallmouth at the upper end may be moving toward their summer locations while those at the lower end are just starting to spawn.

After the nest-guarding and recuperation periods, most smallmouth move to shoreline points and sloping banks where the bottom is composed of rock, gravel, clay or a combination of these materials. Hard-bottomed offshore humps are also prime summertime locations. Typically, the best summertime spots are adjacent to water at least 40 feet deep.

In many cases, smallmouth simply drop deeper on the points and banks where they spawned. If a creek arm is deep enough, smallmouth may stay there all summer rather than moving to the main lake.

The surface temperature of mid-depth reservoirs in the South often exceeds 80°F in summer, so smallmouth are forced to go deep. It is not unusual to catch them at depths of 25 to 35 feet. In the North, typical summertime depths for smallmouth range from 10 to 20 feet.

Flooded timber is not as important to smallmouth as it is to largemouth, but trees and stumps near deep water may hold smallmouth in summer. Timbered flats adjacent to the old river channel often attract fair numbers of smallmouth.

In fall, when the surface temperature drops into the 60s, smallmouth move into shallower water on the same banks, points and humps where they spent the summer. You can find them at depths of 10 to 20 feet until the surface temperature drops below 50°F. Then they begin to move deeper. By late fall, most smallmouth are found deeper than 30 feet. A warm spell in late fall or winter will draw smallmouth much shallower and cause them to start feeding.

Many mid-depth reservoirs undergo a drawdown in fall to increase the storage capacity for spring runoff. When the reservoir is drawn down, the water level may drop as much as 30 feet. In the shallower upper reaches of the lake, smallmouth may have no choice but to retreat to the old river channel or move farther down the lake to find deep water.

Some smallmouth spend the winter in the tailrace of an upstream reservoir, if the reservoir drains from the surface. Smallmouth avoid swift current by nestling behind boulders or staying in eddies.

Seasonal Location in Mid-depth Reservoirs

CREEK ARMS with active inlet streams warm quickly in spring, attracting prespawn smallmouth from the main lake.

ROCK OR GRAVEL SHORELINES, especially those in protected creek arms, make ideal spawning areas.

TIMBERED FLATS along the old river channel are prime nighttime feeding areas for smallmouth in summer.

CURRENT EDGES in the tailrace hold smallmouth all year, but are best from late winter through early summer.

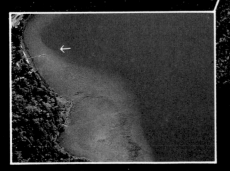

STEEP PORTIONS of a breakline hold more smallmouth in fall than portions that slope

FISH ATTRACTORS made of brush and old tires attract baitfish, which in turn draw

POINTS extending into the old river channel make good summer habitat because

MAIN-LAKE POINTS that are composed of gravel, rock and clay hold smallmouth in summer, fall and winter.

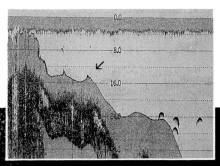

SECONDARY DROP-OFFS on points in creek arms draw smallmouth in summer; primary drop-offs (arrow) in spring.

SUBMERGED ROADBEDS, particularly those built along steep banks, make good feeding areas for smallmouth in summer.

MAIN-LAKE HUMPS that are within easy reach of deep water are likely to draw smallmouth in summer.

FALLEN TREES along steep-sloping banks are good summertime smallmouth spots, much better than trees on gradual slopes.

Shallow Reservoirs

Shallow northern reservoirs, often called flowages, may offer good smallmouth fishing, especially if they have fairly clear water and a rocky basin. Shallow southern reservoirs seldom hold smallmouth; the warm, weedy conditions favor largemouth.

Many shallow reservoirs have extensive areas of flooded timber. The old river channel is often only a few feet deep and there are no significant creek arms. As a result, river and creek channels have less effect on smallmouth movement patterns than in mid-depth reservoirs.

Smallmouth in shallow reservoirs spawn along rocky shorelines and points sheltered from the wind or on offshore reefs. They may spawn in silty bays, if there are enough stumps or logs for cover. Spawning sites range from 2 to 8 feet deep and are almost always near a drop-off.

Prime summertime habitat includes rocky reefs or sand-gravel humps that top off near the surface and slope gradually into deep water. If there are distinct points adjacent to deep water, these also are good summer spots. The best summertime habitat often has some submerged weed growth.

As the surface starts to cool in early fall, smallmouth return to the vicinity of their spawning areas. But when the surface temperature falls into the low 50s, they move to deeper water. They spend the late fall and winter in the old river channel or in other deep areas of the reservoir.

Canyon Reservoirs

Canyon reservoirs sometimes have limited smallmouth populations, but most of these deep, cool impoundments lack the shallow-water cover that smallmouth need. In those that do have smallmouth, the only suitable structure may be submerged ledges along the steep rock walls. In many instances, smallmouth use these ledges through the entire year.

Spawning usually takes place on ledges that are covered with sand or gravel and have boulders for cover. Such ledges are often found at the mouths of inflowing streams. Some smallmouth spawn on gravel shoals in the stream itself. Canyon reservoirs generally have very clear water, so smallmouth may spawn as deep as 20 feet.

After the spawning period, smallmouth drop into slightly deeper water, sometimes suspending just off the spawning ledges. As the water warms, they move progressively deeper. On sunny summer days, you may find them as deep as 80 feet. Smallmouth are drawn to anything along the sheer banks that provides shade. Docks, clumps of brush and rockslides are examples of commonly used cover.

Smallmouth begin to move shallower as the water cools in fall. Often, they return to the same areas where they spawned. Canyon reservoirs in the Southwest remain warm enough that smallmouth continue to feed through the winter.

ROCKY TRIBUTARIES may attract spawning smallmouth if there is a shortage of spawning habitat in the river.

GRAVEL DEPOSITS on inside bends provide good spawning sites. Smallmouth feed on these same bars through fall.

UNDERCUT BANKS, especially those with a lot of exposed roots, are excellent smallmouth spots in summer and fall.

SEASONALLY FLOODED POOLS warm quickly, drawing pre-spawn smallmouth to feed on minnows and insects.

LARGE BOULDERS make it easy to pinpoint eddies where smallmouth feed and rest in summer and fall.

ROCKY POINTS extending into the current also create eddies used by smallmouth in summer and fall.

Small to Medium-Sized Rivers

In many parts of the country, particularly in areas with numerous natural or manmade lakes, small to medium-sized rivers offer a virtually untouched smallmouth-fishing opportunity.

The best rivers have cool, clean water, moderate current (page 141), a winding stream course, and deep pools combined with rock or gravel riffles.

A few weeks before spawning, smallmouth move out of the deep pools where they winter. These pools may be many miles, usually downstream, from the areas where they will spawn and spend the summer. As smallmouth work their way toward their spawning areas, they feed in riffles and along current margins. When not feeding, they drop into the slack water of pools and eddies so they do not have to fight the current.

Shortly after they arrive at their spawning areas, males begin to build nests, usually along the edge of the stream where there is a slight current and a bottom of sand, gravel or rock. Most nests are in 1 to 3 feet of water. If good spawning sites are scarce in

POOLS below riffles hold smallmouth in summer and fall. They feed along the upper lip and rest in the deeper downstream end.

FALLEN TREES and logjams attract minnows and insects and create slack-water pockets. They are best in summer and fall.

SPRINGS attract smallmouth in summer because of their cooler water; in late fall and winter because of their warmer water.

STEEP LEDGES formed where the current cuts into a limestone bank make good smallmouth habitat in summer and fall.

EDDIES alongside the swift water below a dam draw smallmouth after spawning and hold them well into the fall.

DEEP HOLES with no current draw smallmouth from miles away in late fall. They spend the winter in a near-dormant state.

the stream itself, smallmouth may swim up small tributaries to find the right conditions.

After the spawning period, the key to finding smallmouth is to look for current margins where they can rest in slack water and dart into the current to grab drifting food. During this early part of the summer, they remain in fairly shallow water, usually less than 5 feet deep.

By midsummer, most good-sized smallmouth have retreated to deeper pools. The best pools are generally below shallow riffles and have gravel or rock bottoms with boulders, deadfalls, logs, rock ledges or undercut banks for cover. Smallmouth remain in these deeper pools through early fall.

When the water temperature drops into the 60s, smallmouth begin feeding more heavily, usually along current margins similar to those used in early summer. This period of heavy feeding continues until the water temperature drops to the low 50s.

As the water temperature continues to fall, smallmouth move out of the shallows and into the deepest holes. If there are no deep holes in the vicinity of the summer habitat, smallmouth will swim long distances to find the necessary depth, sometimes 10 miles or more. They hold in crevices between rocks or behind any object that shelters them from the current. They stay in these deep holes through winter and feed very little.

Big Rivers

Big rivers that carry only a light silt load may have excellent populations of smallmouth. Such rivers have a diversity of natural and manmade habitat that provides good conditions for spawning, an abundant supply of food, and deep water for winter-ing. But muddy rivers with silt-covered bottoms seldom support many smallmouth.

Most smallmouth winter in deep areas of the main river channel. As the water temperature begins to rise in spring, they leave the deep holes and begin feeding on flats or in eddies along the channel margin, near the locations where they will spawn. Many of them move into areas where the water is warmer, like sloughs off the main channel, or into the mouths of tributaries. Spawning in sloughs and tributaries takes place 1 to 2 weeks earlier than spawning in the main channel.

SHALLOW GRAVEL BARS are commonly used as spawning sites, if the current is not too swift.

BACKWATER AREAS with gravel or riprap shorelines and little current make ideal smallmouth spawning areas.

PILINGS of bridges, piers and docks create small eddies that smallmouth use for summertime feeding and resting areas.

MARINAS warm early and offer lots of cover. Smallmouth move in before spawning and may stay through summer.

TRIBUTARIES that bring in warm water attract smallmouth from spring through early summer.

RIPRAP highway or railroad embankments offer food and cover. They often hold smallmouth from spring through fall.

Prime spawning sites include gravel shorelines, rip-rap banks, and stump fields with a hard bottom. Seldom will smallmouth spawn in midstream, unless there is a boulder or log to afford protection.

Following the spawning period, smallmouth gradually filter out of their spawning areas. They school up in eddies and pools, where they can wait for food to be washed to them rather than waste energy chasing it. They remain in these post-spawn locations through summer.

Examples of good summertime habitat include eddies around islands, wingdams and bridge pilings; rocky pools with some current; eddies below points and inside bends, especially where the water is deep and has lots of rocks or logs for cover; and eddies below dams, riprapped channel markers and rip-rapped lighthouse foundations.

Smallmouth remain in their summer locations until the water temperature drops to about 55°F. Then, they gradually begin to work their way toward the deep holes where they will spend the winter. These holes, 15 to 30 feet deep, are usually located in bends where the water is slack. Big-river smallmouth feed very little from late fall through winter.

ISLANDS with rock or riprap banks are good in summer and fall. Try eddies on the edges and downstream end.

DEEP CUTS connecting the main channel with backwaters concentrate smallmouth in summer and fall.

CHANNEL MARKERS are often placed on manmade rock piles. The downstream eddies hold smallmouth in summer and fall.

EDDIES downstream from points hold smallmouth in summer and fall. Floating debris helps pinpoint the eddies.

WINGDAMS are prime smallmouth feeding areas in summer and fall. Active smallmouth usually lie along the upstream lip.

DEEP HOLES in the main river channel provide protection from the current and draw smallmouth in late fall and winter.

Prime Smallmouth Waters

Although the smallmouth's native range included only the eastern half of the United States and extreme southeastern Canada, widespread stocking has put good smallmouth fishing within easy reach of the majority of North American anglers.

To determine the best smallmouth-fishing waters in North America, Hunting & Fishing Library researchers conducted a poll of state and provincial natural-resources agencies and expert fishermen. The most productive waters in each of the major smallmouth-fishing regions are shown below.

NORTHERN NATURAL LAKES REGION. This region produces more smallmouth bass than anywhere else in the world. Laced among thousands of cool, clear glacial lakes that hold smallmouth are thousands of miles of smallmouth rivers and streams. Although the Great Lakes are in this region, they will be discussed separately on pages 72-73.

Most of the lakes in the northern portion of this region are cold and infertile, falling into either the

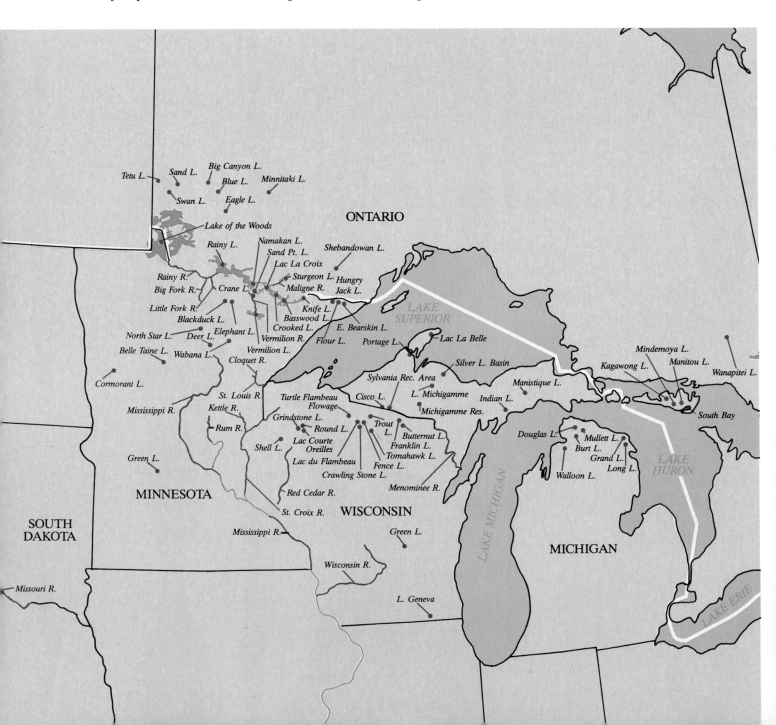

oligotrophic (pages 54 to 57) or mesotrophic (pages 50 to 53) categories. In the southern portion of the region, most of the lakes are mesotrophic or eutrophic (page 58).

Many waters in the northern portion are located in wilderness areas, like the Boundary Waters Canoe Area Wilderness in northern Minnesota and the Quetico Provincial Park in southwestern Ontario. Access to these waters is limited; many can be reached only by portaging a canoe. Even though they are not as productive as waters farther south, they receive very light fishing pressure, so catches of 50 to 100 smallmouth a day are not unusual.

The region has a tremendous diversity of smallmouth waters ranging from 100-acre unnamed lakes to Lake of the Woods, which covers nearly 1 million acres. In the western part of the region, most anglers pursue walleyes and northern pike, so smallmouth are often overlooked. In many lakes in the eastern part, smallmouth take a back seat to trout and landlocked salmon.

Because the waters are so diverse, the best fishing times vary widely. But in most cases, fishing is good from late May through mid-July and from September through early October.

Smallmouth in this region generally run from 1½ to 2½ pounds and top off at about 7 pounds. Excluding fish caught in the Great Lakes, the largest smallmouth ever taken in the region was a 9 pound, 4 ounce fish caught in Long Lake, Michigan in 1950.

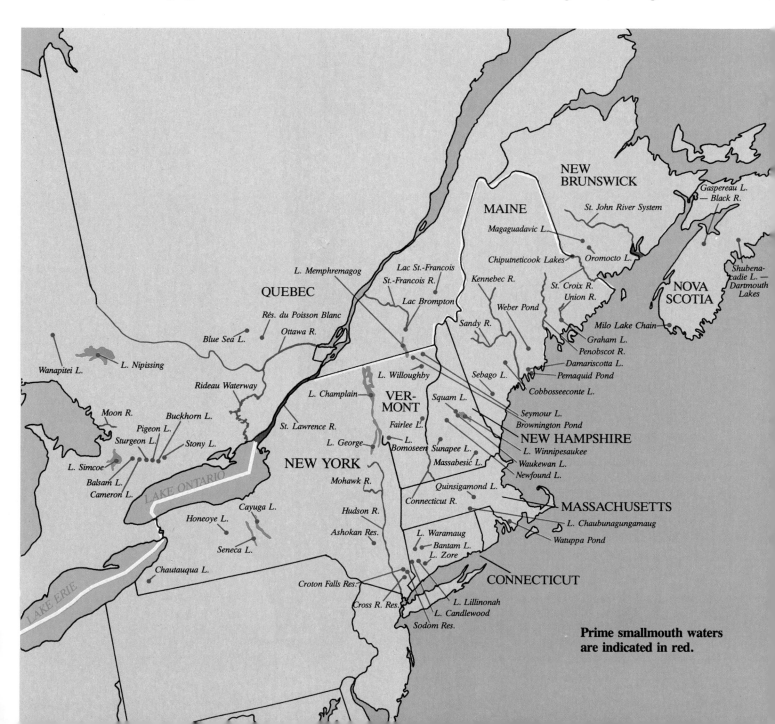

Prime smallmouth waters are indicated in red.

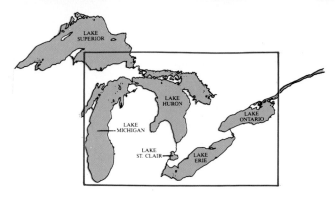

GREAT LAKES. The shallow, warmwater portions of the Great Lakes offer excellent smallmouth fishing, as do many of the connecting rivers, canals and smaller lakes. The deep, open waters of the Great Lakes are too cold for smallmouth.

There are several reasons for the top-rate smallmouth bass fishing in the Great Lakes and their connecting waters:

· Because of the vast expanses of water, the Great Lakes have the capacity to produce huge numbers of smallmouth.

· Compared to the trout, salmon, walleye and yellow perch fishing, the smallmouth fishing has drawn little attention.

· Unlike walleyes and lake trout, smallmouth have not been harvested by commercial fishermen.

Throughout most of the Great Lakes, the best smallmouth fishing is found in shallow, warmwater bays and around islands and shallow underwater reefs. The deep waters are better suited to trout, salmon and other coldwater species.

Some islands and reefs in the Great Lakes are so isolated that they are seldom fished. But anglers who are willing to travel 30 miles or more by boat can enjoy some of the finest trophy-smallmouth fishing to be found anywhere.

The best-known smallmouth-fishing area in the Great Lakes is the Bass Islands area in Lake Erie. Although this area has been fished heavily for many years, it continues to produce impressive numbers of good-sized smallmouth.

Fishing in shallow, warmwater bays and connecting rivers and canals is generally best from late April through June. Around main-lake reefs and islands, smallmouth bite best from mid-June until early August. For those willing to brave the weather, main-lake fishing can also be good from September to early November.

A typical Great Lakes smallmouth weighs from 1½ to 3 pounds, but 5- to 6-pounders are taken with surprising regularity by anglers familiar with the waters. In 1964, one of the largest smallmouth ever recorded was caught in Lake Ontario. It weighed 11 pounds, 8 ounces.

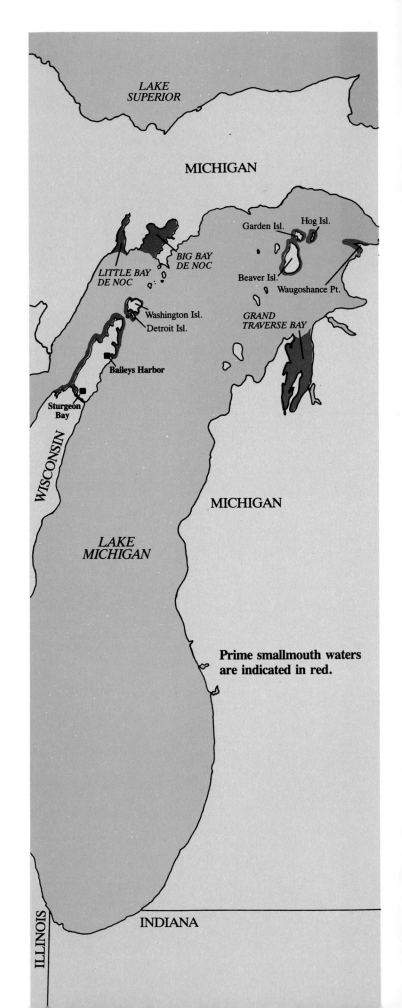

Prime smallmouth waters are indicated in red.

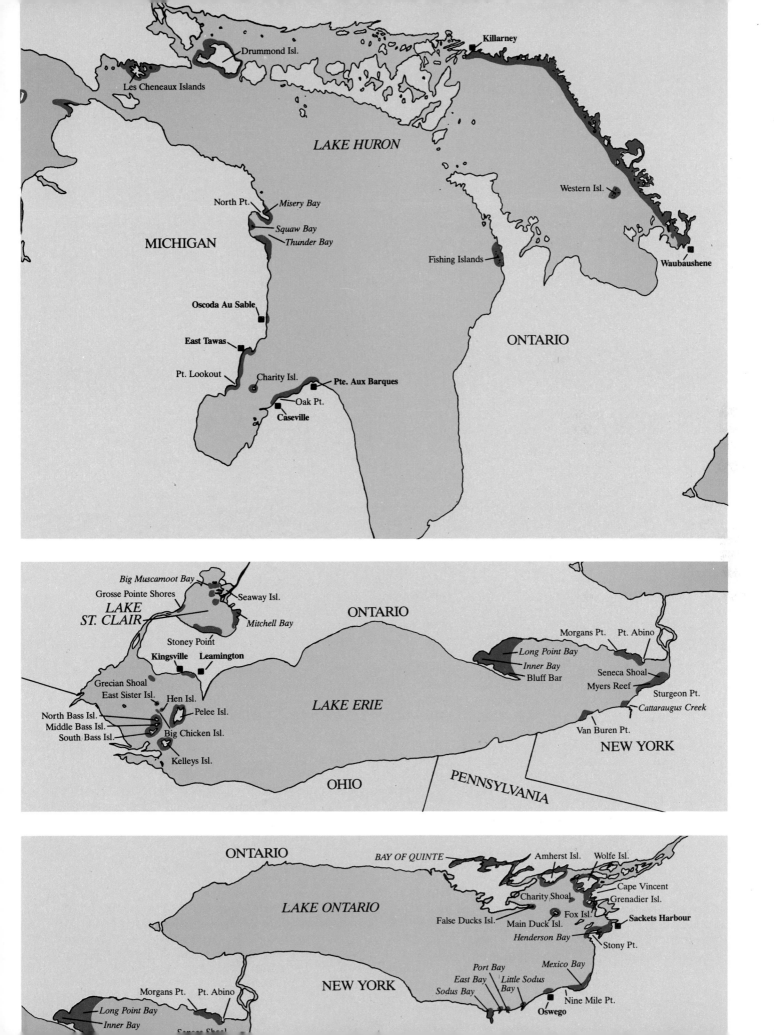

LAKE HURON

Drummond Isl.

Les Cheneaux Islands

Killarney

Western Isl.

MICHIGAN

North Pt. — *Misery Bay*

Squaw Bay

Thunder Bay

Fishing Islands

Waubaushene

Oscoda Au Sable

ONTARIO

East Tawas

Pt. Lookout

Charity Isl.

Pte. Aux Barques

Oak Pt.

Caseville

Big Muscamoot Bay

Grosse Pointe Shores

Seaway Isl.

**LAKE
ST. CLAIR**

Mitchell Bay

ONTARIO

Morgans Pt.   Pt. Abino

Stoney Point

Long Point Bay

Kingsville   **Leamington**

Inner Bay

Bluff Bar

Seneca Shoal

Grecian Shoal

Myers Reef

East Sister Isl.

Hen Isl.

Sturgeon Pt.

North Bass Isl.

Pelee Isl.

Cattaraugus Creek

LAKE ERIE

Middle Bass Isl.

South Bass Isl.

Big Chicken Isl.

Van Buren Pt.

NEW YORK

Kelleys Isl.

OHIO   **PENNSYLVANIA**

ONTARIO

BAY OF QUINTE

Amherst Isl.   Wolfe Isl.

Charity Shoal

Cape Vincent

LAKE ONTARIO

Grenadier Isl.

Fox Isl.

False Ducks Isl.

Main Duck Isl.

Sackets Harbour

Henderson Bay

Stony Pt.

Port Bay   *Mexico Bay*

Morgans Pt.   Pt. Abino

East Bay   *Little Sodus
Bay*

Long Point Bay

Sodus Bay

Nine Mile Pt.

NEW YORK

Oswego

Inner Bay

Seneca Shoal

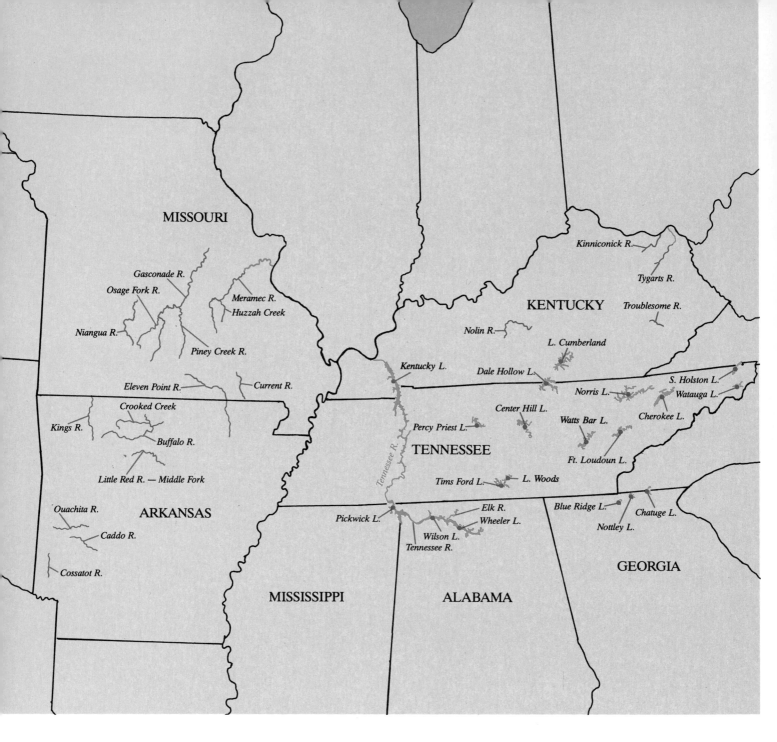

MID-SOUTH RESERVOIR REGION. These waters produce the world's biggest smallmouth. In addition to the world-record smallmouth weighing 11 pounds, 15 ounces, several other smallmouth over 10 pounds have been caught in this region.

The best mid-south reservoirs are in mountainous areas, and have plenty of deep, cool water. Shallower reservoirs in the region have few smallmouth because the water is too warm in summer.

Most mid-south reservoirs have super-abundant crops of shad. The excellent food supply combined with the long growing season account for the large size of the smallmouth. In addition, most southern anglers concentrate on largemouth, so smallmouth receive less fishing pressure.

Smallmouth fishing in this region peaks in March and April, slows during the warm summer months, then picks up again in September and stays good through November. In summer, you can catch some smallmouth by fishing at night. Stringers of 3- to 4-pound smallmouth are fairly common in this region, and 5- to 7-pounders are not unusual.

Although the reservoirs get the most attention, many rivers in the Ozark and Ouachita Mountains also have good smallmouth populations. The best fishing is in remote areas where access is limited.

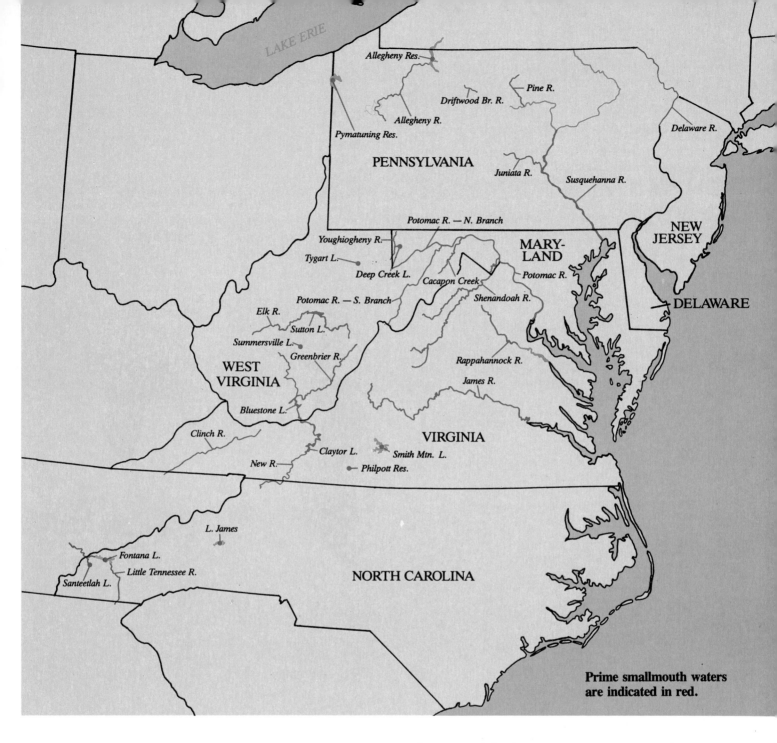

Prime smallmouth waters are indicated in red.

EASTERN RIVERS REGION. Historically famous for its smallmouth fishing, this region continues to provide quality angling despite heavy fishing pressure. Smallmouth fishing is actually improving in some rivers because of stricter water quality standards.

Originally, smallmouth were found only in the Ohio River drainage system. But widespread stocking has established smallmouth in virtually every major river system in the region.

The best smallmouth rivers in this region are in hilly or mountainous country where difficult access keeps fishing pressure to a minimum.

Smallmouth in the northern part of the region begin to bite in March; those in the southern part in April. Fishing remains good through October.

In the northern part, smallmouth generally run 1 to 2 pounds, with an occasional 4- to 5-pounder. They grow larger in the southern part, averaging 2 to 3 pounds with a few in the 6- to 7-pound class.

While the vast majority of smallmouth in the eastern rivers region are caught in rivers and streams, some of the deeper, colder reservoirs also have good numbers of smallmouth. The Hiwassee Reservoir in North Carolina produced a 10 pound, 2 ounce smallmouth in 1953.

MIDWESTERN RIVERS REGION. Because of the heavy agricultural use of this region, most of the lakes have silted in and become too fertile for smallmouth. But many rivers and streams have fair to good smallmouth fishing.

The upper reaches of the rivers usually offer the best smallmouth fishing because the water is clear and cool, and the bottom free of silt. Farther downstream, the rivers carry more silt and may be too warm.

In some spring-fed streams, the cold upper reaches hold trout, the cool middle reaches have smallmouth, and the warm lower reaches support only roughfish like carp and bullheads.

Smallmouth in midwestern rivers and streams begin to bite in mid- to late April. The best fishing is usually in May and June, although some smallmouth are caught through October. Smallmouth in these waters average 1 to 2 pounds with an occasional fish topping 5 pounds.

Many of the lakes in this region have heavy algal blooms and are too silty to support smallmouth. But a few have a limited smallmouth fishery. Because of the minimal quantity of smallmouth and the abundance of food in these fertile lakes, fishing is usually difficult. But when you catch a smallmouth, it is likely to be a big one.

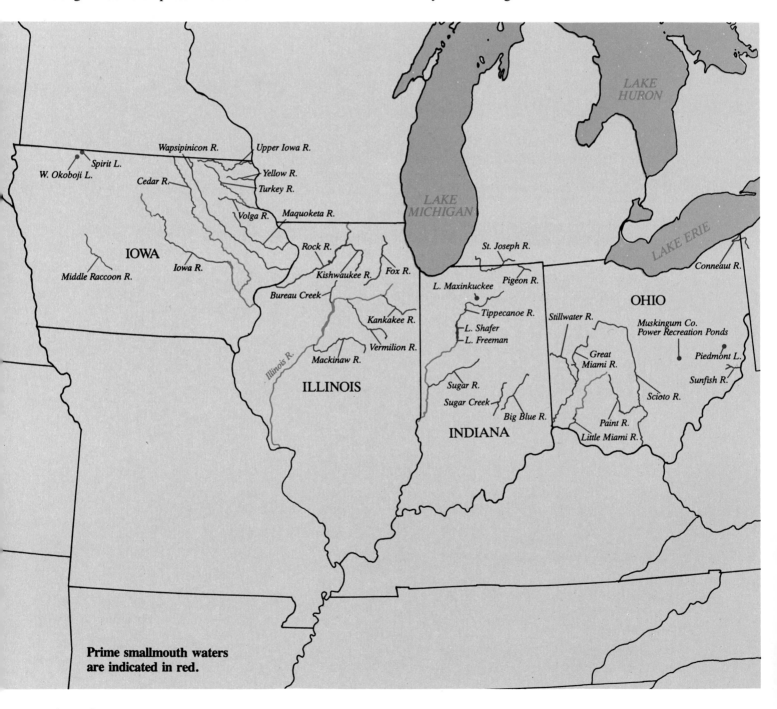

Prime smallmouth waters are indicated in red.

NORTHERN CALIFORNIA RESERVOIRS. The rivers feeding these reservoirs were stocked with smallmouth in the early 1900s. When the rivers were dammed, smallmouth began to proliferate in the reservoirs and are now providing some outstanding fishing. Some of these deep, clear reservoirs have trout and salmon in the depths and smallmouth in the warmer, shallower water.

Fishing is best from mid-March through April and from mid-August through mid-October. Most of the smallmouth range from 1½ to 3 pounds. The Claire Engle Reservoir produced a 9 pound, 1 ounce smallmouth in 1976.

SOUTHWESTERN RESERVOIRS. Like northern California reservoirs, these steep-sided canyon reservoirs often have trout in the depths and smallmouth in the shallower portions. Some shallower reservoirs and a few rivers in the Southwest have also been stocked with smallmouth and are producing good fishing.

Fishing is generally best from December through March. Night fishing can be good from May through July, but the fish generally do not run as large.

Smallmouth in this region typically weigh from 1 to 3 pounds with an occasional 6-pounder.

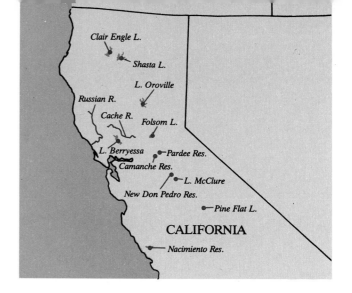

PACIFIC NORTHWEST. Trout and salmon are the primary targets of anglers in this region, so smallmouth receive very little attention. But good smallmouth populations are present in major rivers such as the Columbia and Snake and in some of their larger tributaries.

The smallmouth start to bite in spring, as soon as the rivers recede and clear up. Fishing remains good through July. September and October are also good times. Most of the smallmouth run from 1½ to 2 pounds, but several 10 to 11 pounders have been taken by survey crews while shocking in the Columbia River in Washington.

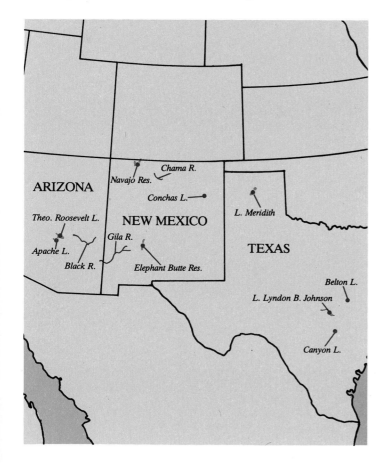

Basic Smallmouth-Fishing Techniques

OBJECT FISHING is effective when smallmouth are in the shallows. Motor along slowly, looking for boulders, logs, stumps, brush piles or any other visible object that provides shade. Cast as close to the object as possible, making sure to work the shady side. Wear polarized glasses so you can see objects below the surface. Do not spend too much time in one spot; the active fish will usually bite on the first or second cast.

Smallmouth-Fishing Fundamentals

To catch smallmouth bass consistently, you must understand a few basic fishing principles that always apply, regardless of the technique you use.

· Smallmouth are object-oriented, meaning that they like to get next to something. Their favorite type of object is a large rock. They are sometimes found around weeds, but are not as weed-oriented as largemouth.

· In a given body of water, smallmouth can usually be found deeper than largemouth, but shallower than walleye.

· Smallmouth school by size, so if you are catching nothing but small ones, try a different area.

· Smallmouth have different personalities in different waters. In high-competition waters (pages 30-31), they tend to be aggressive, so a variety of presentations will work. But in low-competition waters, they can be very finicky. Here, a slow, tantalizing presentation draws the most strikes.

· Small-sized smallmouth are more aggressive than large ones and generally inhabit shallower water.

· Smallmouth are prone to spooking, even in waters where they are normally aggressive.

· Most smallmouth are caught near the bottom, but you can also catch them on the surface. However, they are not as vulnerable to surface presentations as largemouth.

· In most waters, smallmouth bite best in early morning. In clear lakes, they may bite best at night, especially in summer.

SELECT small lures and baits when fishing for smallmouth bass. A smallmouth (top) would prefer a 4-inch plastic worm, for instance, while a largemouth (bottom) would prefer a 7-inch worm.

KEEP a low profile to avoid spooking smallmouth. Pay attention to the sun so you do not cast your shadow over the fish. Keep your movement to a minimum and do not drop anything on the bottom of the boat.

Boat Control

One of the biggest problems for the average fisherman is learning to control his boat. The wind and current constantly seem to work against him. So he spends too much time fishing in unproductive water or presenting his bait at the wrong speed.

The smallmouth's skittishness makes boat control even more important, especially in clear water. If you are casting to a shallow reef, for instance, and allow your boat to drift too close, you may as well look for a new fishing spot.

Once you locate the fish, the objective of most boat-control techniques is to keep the boat at a precise depth. To accomplish this, a depth finder is essential. Expert fishermen keep their eyes glued to their depth finders.

You can control your boat much easier with a tiller than with a steering wheel. A tiller allows you to steer and operate the throttle with one hand, leaving the other hand free for fishing. And you can turn more quickly with a tiller, so you can make a faster adjustment when the depth changes.

Ideally, you should have an electric motor in addition to your outboard. With an electric motor matched to your boat, you can maneuver in all but the windiest weather. Many smallmouth fishermen have two electric motors, one mounted on the bow and one on the transom. The bow-mount works better for some techniques, like motoring along a shoreline while casting into the shallows. The transom-mount is a better choice for backtrolling.

Smallmouth fishermen should become familiar with the following boat-control techniques:

Trolling

To most fishermen, trolling means motoring forward slowly while pulling their line behind the boat. By trolling forward, you can go fast enough to troll with crankbaits and other fast-moving lures. When forward trolling, fishermen in the front of the boat must be careful to keep their line from tangling in the propeller.

It is difficult to present live bait and some types of lures slowly enough by trolling forward, so you should also know how to backtroll.

Backtrolling enables you to move more slowly because outboard motors are geared lower in reverse. Also, the transom becomes the leading end, and its flat surface has more water resistance than the bow.

Another big advantage to backtrolling is the ease of following an exact depth contour (see below). And wind has less effect on the transom than on the bow, so you are less likely to be blown off course. When trolling forward, you cannot make depth corrections as quickly.

How Backtrolling Makes Depth Control Easier

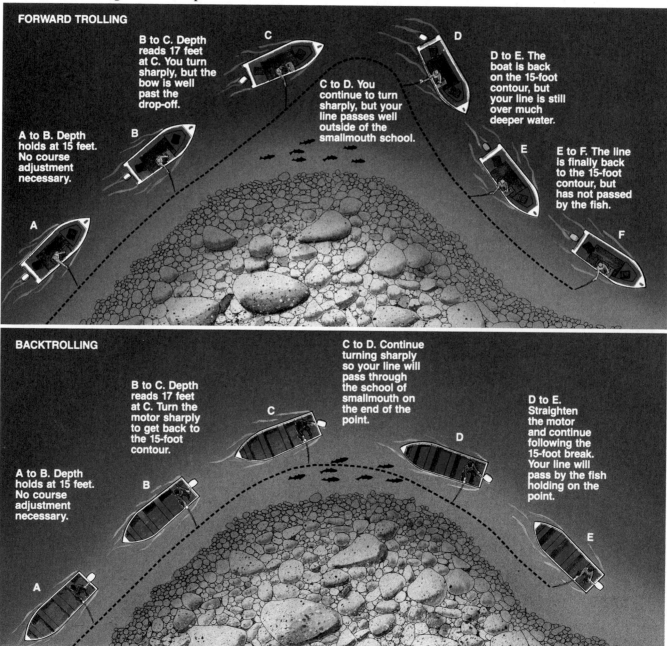

FORWARD TROLLING

A to B. Depth holds at 15 feet. No course adjustment necessary.

B to C. Depth reads 17 feet at C. You turn sharply, but the bow is well past the drop-off.

C to D. You continue to turn sharply, but your line passes well outside of the smallmouth school.

D to E. The boat is back on the 15-foot contour, but your line is still over much deeper water.

E to F. The line is finally back to the 15-foot contour, but has not passed by the fish.

BACKTROLLING

A to B. Depth holds at 15 feet. No course adjustment necessary.

B to C. Depth reads 17 feet at C. Turn the motor sharply to get back to the 15-foot contour.

C to D. Continue turning sharply so your line will pass through the school of smallmouth on the end of the point.

D to E. Straighten the motor and continue following the 15-foot break. Your line will pass by the fish holding on the point.

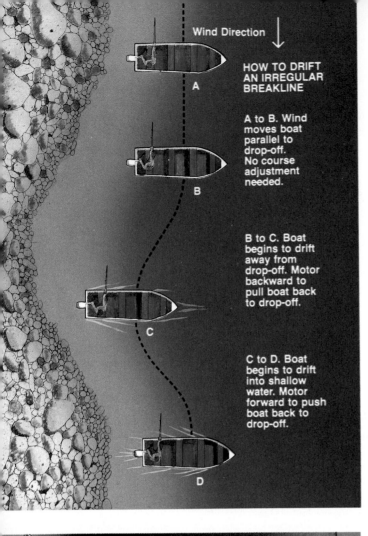

Wind Direction ↓

HOW TO DRIFT AN IRREGULAR BREAKLINE

A to B. Wind moves boat parallel to drop-off. No course adjustment needed.

B to C. Boat begins to drift away from drop-off. Motor backward to pull boat back to drop-off.

C to D. Boat begins to drift into shallow water. Motor forward to push boat back to drop-off.

Drifting

The major advantage to drifting is that you do not have to run your motor continuously and risk spooking the fish. If you need to make course adjustments as you drift, an electric trolling motor will do the job.

Drifting is generally not recommended in water less than 10 feet deep because smallmouth often spook at the sight of a moving boat or from its shadow, even if the motor is not running.

Drifting works well in still or moving water. In still water, you can drift along a breakline or make a series of parallel drifts to cover a reef. In current, you can drift along while casting to likely cover or jigging vertically.

When the wind exceeds 15 miles per hour, your drift speed will probably be too fast. To solve this problem, attach a sea anchor to the bow or drag a heavy chain off the side of the boat (page 142). Or, use your motor to slow your drift as described in the section on slipping (below).

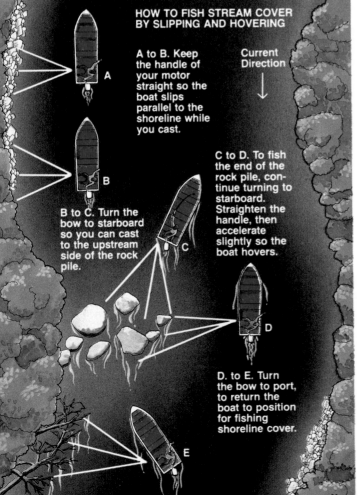

HOW TO FISH STREAM COVER BY SLIPPING AND HOVERING

A to B. Keep the handle of your motor straight so the boat slips parallel to the shoreline while you cast.

Current Direction ↓

B to C. Turn the bow to starboard so you can cast to the upstream side of the rock pile.

C to D. To fish the end of the rock pile, continue turning to starboard. Straighten the handle, then accelerate slightly so the boat hovers.

D. to E. Turn the bow to port, to return the boat to position for fishing shoreline cover.

Slipping and Hovering

Slipping means running your motor against the wind or current to slow your drift. The boat still moves in the direction of the wind or current, but you can present your bait more slowly and work likely spots more thoroughly than you could by drifting.

Because of the counteracting forces, slipping is a difficult technique to perfect. In a river, the safest method is to point the bow into the current and run the motor in forward; in a lake, some fishermen prefer to point the transom into the wind and run the motor in reverse.

By running your motor at the speed that exactly counteracts the wind or current, you can hold the boat nearly motionless while working a likely spot. This technique is called *hovering*.

The biggest problem in perfecting the slipping technique is learning to steer. The basic concept is to steer as if the boat were moving ahead, even though it is slipping backwards.

Anchoring

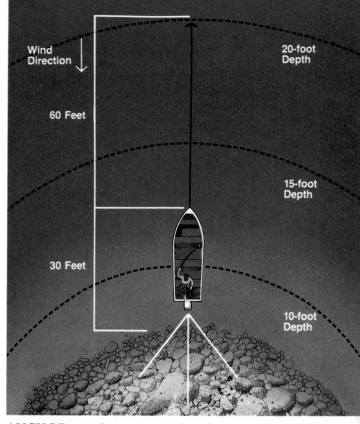

When you find a school of smallmouth, or when you suspect smallmouth are concentrated in a relatively small area, anchor your boat. Anchoring allows you to work the school more thoroughly and to use techniques that would otherwise be difficult, like slip-bobber fishing. And anchoring is often the only practical way to control your boat in strong winds.

When smallmouth are skittish, anchoring is the best boat-control technique. If you repeatedly troll or drift over a school in shallow water, you may catch a fish or two, but you could probably catch a dozen or more by anchoring.

But anchoring is effective only when done properly. For instance, if you pull up on a shallow reef, throw out your anchor with a big splash, and let it clank down on the rocks, you will send smallmouth scurrying to the depths. Instead, quietly lower your anchor in deep water and let the wind position the boat so you can cast to the reef. Carry an anchor heavy enough to insure that it does not slip.

ANCHOR your boat securely by using an anchor rope at least three times as long as the water is deep. To anchor within casting distance of this reef, motor about 90 feet upwind where the water is 20 feet deep. Then drop anchor and let out about 60 feet of rope.

How to Work a Reef from One Anchor Position

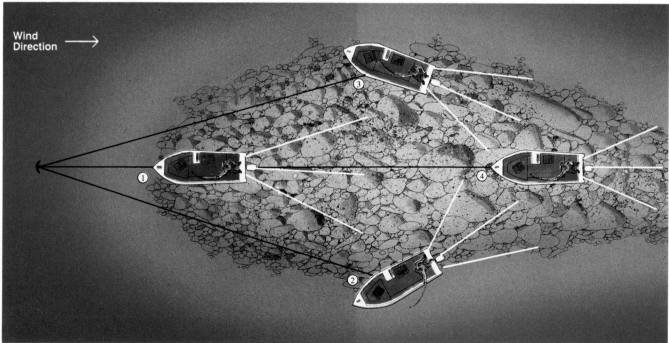

DROP ANCHOR far enough upwind of the reef so you can work the upwind portion with the anchor rope tied to (1) the bow eye. To work one side of the reef, let out some more rope and tie it to a cleat near (2) the starboard bow. The side of the boat acts as a sail, so instead of riding directly downwind of the anchor, the boat swings to port. To work the other side of the reef, tie the rope to a cleat near (3) the port bow; the boat will swing to starboard. To work the downwind side, let out more rope and attach it to (4) the bow eye.

How to Play a Smallmouth

The aerial acrobatics of a good-sized smallmouth can humble even the most experienced fisherman. When a smallmouth grabs your bait, then rockets out of the water shaking its head, the hook often comes flying back at you.

Everyone is going to lose some smallmouth. There is no way to avoid it. But there are some things you can do to increase the percentage of smallmouth that you land:

· Avoid using a stiff, fast-action rod, unless you are experienced at playing hard-fighting fish. A rod with slower action bends over more of its length, so it is more forgiving of mistakes in playing the fish. The drawback to a slower action is that you will have more trouble setting the hook.

· Be sure to test your drag before you start fishing. When a smallmouth strikes and starts making a run, there will not be enough time to tinker with your drag.

- If you use spinning tackle, you may want to tighten your drag so it does not slip at all. A tight drag gives you a stronger hook set. With the drag tight, you must keep the anti-reverse mechanism disengaged and fight the fish by *backreeling*. You do not have to rely on the drag, so you will never lose a fish because the drag sticks. But the technique requires a great deal of experience in playing fish because you must immediately reel backwards when the smallmouth makes a run.

- Set the hook hard. Some fishermen set the hook two or three times to be sure the barb is sunk.

- Keep your line tight. One of the smallmouth's favorite tricks is to take your bait in deep water, then bolt for the surface, leaving you with pile of slack line. If you see your line coming up, reel rapidly to take up the slack. Otherwise, the fish will probably throw the hook when it jumps.

- Play the smallmouth out before bringing it close to the boat. If you horse the fish in while it is still *green,* it is more likely to throw the hook or break your line. Fighting the fish at a distance gives you more margin for error because of the increased line stretch.

Tips on Playing Smallmouth

BACKREEL at once when the smallmouth makes a run. Fight the fish with your rod tip high. If you keep your rod tip pointed at the fish, a sudden run could snap the line.

LET GO of the reel handle if the fish swims so fast you cannot backreel. To keep your line from snarling, feather the spool so it cannot turn after the fish stops running.

DROP your rod tip at the moment the smallmouth jumps, especially when it is close to the boat. By dropping the rod tip, you reduce the line tension enough to prevent a break-off.

Tips on Landing and Releasing Smallmouth

LIP-LAND a smallmouth by grabbing its lower jaw with your thumb inside its mouth. Do not attempt to lip-land a smallmouth that has been hooked on a crankbait or any other lure with more than one treble hook.

RELEASE the smallmouth by gently setting it back in the water, rather than throwing it. If you plan on releasing a fish that has swallowed the bait, clip the line rather than attempting to dislodge the hook.

Fishing with Artificial Lures

Smallmouth will strike almost any type of artificial lure, as long as it is similar in size to the food they normally eat. One of the most common mistakes in smallmouth fishing is using lures that are too big.

Most smallmouth are taken on lures from 2 to 4 inches long. Even trophy smallmouth prefer lures in that size range. Larger lures work better only in late fall, when the size of the natural food has increased, or at night.

A 6-inch minnow plug is a popular lure for largemouth bass, but is seldom a good choice for smallmouth. Although smallmouth occasionally will take a plug this long, a 3-inch model would be a more consistent producer.

Similarly, the ⅜- to ½-ounce spinnerbaits that work so well for largemouth are usually a poor choice for smallmouth. A ⅛-ounce spinnerbait would be much more effective.

Generally, smallmouth prefer dark or natural colors to bright, gaudy ones. For most other gamefish, the clarity of the water is an important factor in choosing lure colors. So fishermen carry a wide selection of lures, including bright or fluorescent ones for fishing in murky water. But most smallmouth waters are relatively clear, so this wide selection may not be necessary. Bright lures often work well during the spawning period, however, because the bass are aggressive and not easily spooked.

Smallmouth anglers should not rely on electronic color-selecting devices. These devices tell you what color is most visible to fish, not what color they are most inclined to strike. In many cases, a gaudy,

highly visible lure actually seems to spook smallmouth rather than attract them.

Experienced anglers know that smallmouth are particularly vulnerable to a stop-and-go retrieve. In most cases, smallmouth strike as soon as you stop reeling. This habit was confirmed in a laboratory study on predator-prey relationships. Researchers found that smallmouth usually attacked their prey immediately after it stopped swimming.

During periods of heavy runoff and low water clarity, noisy lures seem to work best. One of the best choices in this situation is a vibrating plug with a rattle chamber. Another effective lure is a spinner with a larger-than-normal blade for extra vibration.

Fishing with Jigs

If you were limited to only one lure for all of your smallmouth fishing, your best choice would undoubtedly be a lead-head jig. A jig will catch smallmouth in any type of water at any time of year. And you can work a jig through practically any type of cover and at any depth where smallmouth are likely to be found.

JIGGING BASICS. Jig fishing for smallmouth is much like jig fishing for largemouth or walleyes. Smallmouth generally strike as the jig is sinking, so you must keep a taut line at this critical stage. If you let the line go slack as the jig sinks, you will probably not feel the strike.

Even with a taut line, smallmouth strikes may be difficult to feel. In cold water or whenever a smallmouth is not in the mood to feed, it swims up to a jig and simply closes its mouth on it. You may feel a little extra weight, or the line may go slack or move slightly to the side. If you do not set the hook quickly, the smallmouth will spit the jig.

Detecting these subtle strikes is much easier with a sensitive rod. A 5¼- to 6-foot, fast-action, medium-power graphite spinning rod designed for 6- to 8-pound mono is a good all-around choice. For casting tiny jigs around shallow cover, many anglers prefer a 5- to 5½-foot ultralight graphite spinning rod with 4- to 6-pound mono.

The way you work your jig depends on the time of year and the mood of the smallmouth. During cold-water periods, a gentle twitch or slow lift is usually more effective than a sharp snap. But in warm water, a sharp snap may work better.

Because smallmouth prefer subtle colors, some expert fishermen use unpainted jig heads. The gray color has a natural minnow-like look, especially when the jig is tipped with a smoke-, amber- or motor oil-colored grub tail. Other popular jig colors are black, brown, white and green. Bright or fluorescent colors are used mainly in murky water and around spawning time.

In most situations, tipping your jig with live bait is not necessary. In fact, tipping may result in fewer smallmouth because they tend to strike short. But tipping will probably improve your success at water temperatures below 55°F, in low-competition waters and under cold-front conditions.

Instead of live bait, many experts use a 2-inch pork strip for tipping their jigs. A pork strip has a true-to-life action and is nearly impossible to tear off the hook. Most pork strips are designed for largemouth

How Smallmouth Take a Jig

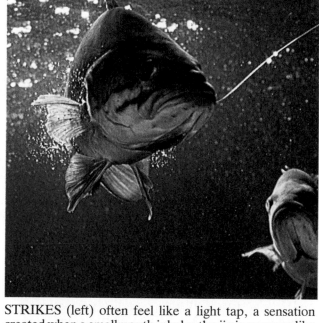

STRIKES (left) often feel like a light tap, a sensation created when a smallmouth inhales the jig in vacuum-like fashion. If it detects something unnatural, a smallmouth expels the jig (right) within a fraction of a second. Experienced fishermen know they must set the hook instantly at any hint of a strike.

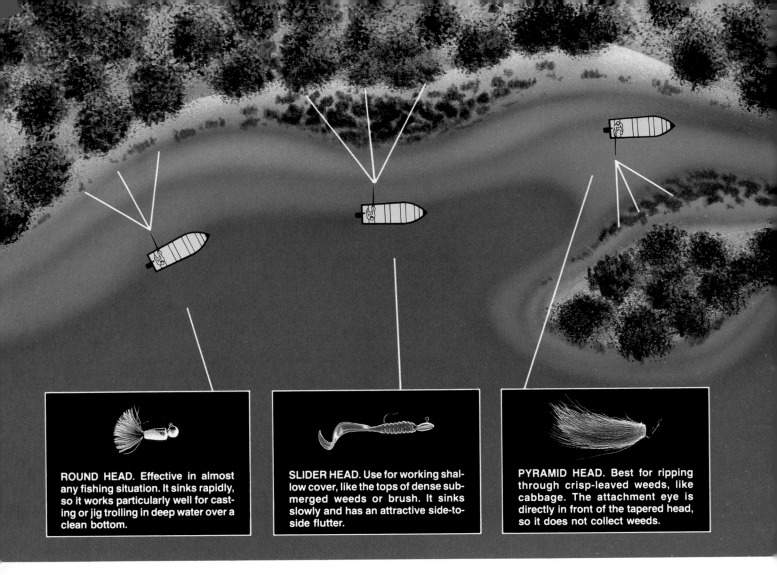

ROUND HEAD. Effective in almost any fishing situation. It sinks rapidly, so it works particularly well for casting or jig trolling in deep water over a clean bottom.

SLIDER HEAD. Use for working shallow cover, like the tops of dense submerged weeds or brush. It sinks slowly and has an attractive side-to-side flutter.

PYRAMID HEAD. Best for ripping through crisp-leaved weeds, like cabbage. The attachment eye is directly in front of the tapered head, so it does not collect weeds.

and are too big for smallmouth, so you have to cut them to size.

Versatile smallmouth fishermen use several different jig-fishing techniques, including casting, jig trolling and vertical jigging. Each technique has its advantages and disadvantages.

CASTING. Casting with a jig is extremely effective in a wide variety of smallmouth-fishing situations.

When smallmouth are holding in the shade of rocks, logs or other objects, cast a jig and let it sink into their hiding spot. Often, a smallmouth will grab the jig before it hits bottom.

To catch smallmouth in stream pools or eddies, cast a jig into the slack water. It will sink into the fish zone before the current sweeps it away.

When smallmouth are scattered along a breakline, drift or slowly motor along just out from it, cast a jig into the shallows, then retrieve down the drop-off.

To work a specific piece of structure, like a sharp point or small reef, anchor your boat and cast. If you suspect the smallmouth are in shallow water, anchor in deep water, cast into the shallows and retrieve downhill. You will need a long rope to make the anchor hold. If the fish are deep, anchor in the shallows and retrieve uphill, or anchor along the drop-off and retrieve parallel to the break.

For casting into shallow water, use a slow-sinking jig. A slower sink rate is more attractive to smallmouth and results in fewer snags. Use a ⅟₁₆- to ⅛-ounce jig in depths of 10 feet or less. Some fishermen use a slider-type jig with a buoyant dressing. Others mold their own jig heads using tin instead of lead. Smallmouth like the shine of the tin head and the sink rate is much slower than that of a lead head.

JIG TROLLING. This technique has not gained widespread popularity, but is one of the best ways to locate smallmouth. It enables you to cover a lot of territory while keeping your jig in the most productive depth range.

The technique works best in water of moderate depth, usually from 12 to 20 feet. In shallower water, jig trolling may spook smallmouth; in deeper water, you may have trouble maintaining bottom contact.

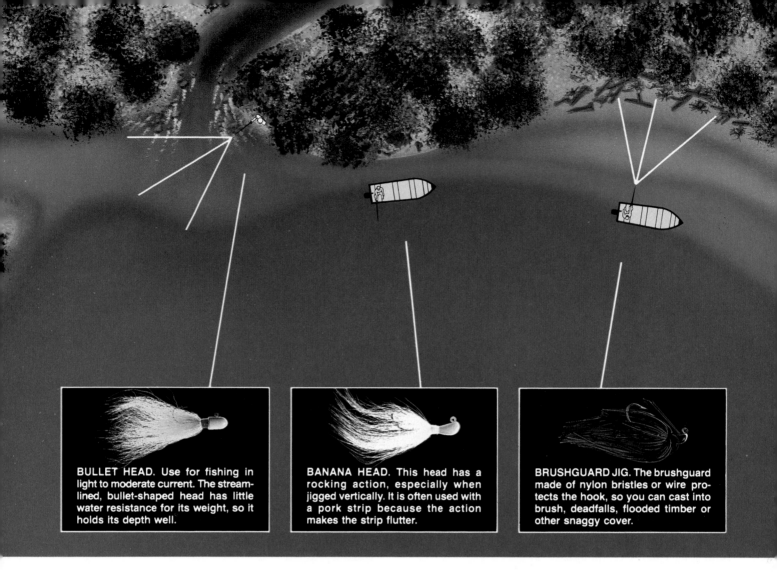

BULLET HEAD. Use for fishing in light to moderate current. The streamlined, bullet-shaped head has little water resistance for its weight, so it holds its depth well.

BANANA HEAD. This head has a rocking action, especially when jigged vertically. It is often used with a pork strip because the action makes the strip flutter.

BRUSHGUARD JIG. The brushguard made of nylon bristles or wire protects the hook, so you can cast into brush, deadfalls, flooded timber or other snaggy cover.

Jig trolling requires moving the boat very slowly while precisely following a contour. The best way to control your speed and depth is to backtroll with an electric motor.

To begin jig trolling, lower your jig to bottom. Let out only enough line so your jig can touch. Repeatedly lift the jig and lower it until you see the line go slack. Being able to see your line go slack after each jigging stroke is the key to successful jig trolling.

If you troll into deeper water, you will lose bottom contact, so the line will not go slack. Let out just enough line to reach bottom, then continue trolling. If you troll into shallower water, too much line will drag on bottom. You will not see your line go slack because the jig does not lift off bottom even though you are lifting your rod. The best solution is to reel in your jig, then start over.

A round-head jig is a good choice for jig trolling because it sinks rapidly, enabling you to feel bottom easily. Use a ⅛- to ¼-ounce jig in depths down to 20 feet. In deeper water or in windy weather, you may need a ⅜-ounce jig. Avoid using bulky bucktail or large soft-plastic dressings that reduce the sink rate, making it difficult to maintain bottom contact.

VERTICAL JIGGING. One of the best deep-water techniques, vertical jigging is especially effective in late fall and winter, when smallmouth commonly retreat to depths of 30 to 50 feet and form tight schools. In summer, vertical jigging works well in waters of low to moderate clarity.

Working a jig in deep water requires hovering over a specific spot while jigging straight up and down. On a calm day, keeping the boat stationary is no problem. But on a windy day, you must point the transom of your boat into the wind, put your motor into reverse, and adjust the throttle to compensate for the wind.

If you are accustomed to jig fishing and have a sensitive touch, you can get by with a jig as light as ¼ ounce. But most fishermen use ⅜- to ½-ounce jigs for vertical jigging.

Because of line stretch at these extreme depths, detecting strikes may be difficult. Low-stretch line makes it easier to feel a slight tap or nudge.

How to Tip a Jig with Live Bait

TIP a jig with a minnow by hooking it (1) through the lips, (2) through the eyes or (3) through the mouth and out just behind the head. Hook a crawler (4) through the middle or (5) by threading it on so it trails naturally. Hook a leech (6) through the sucker end; a crayfish tail (7) through the broken end, so the hook point comes out through the back; and a hellgrammite (8) through the mouth and out the back.

How to Tip a Jig with Pork Rind

CUT a piece of pork rind that is too big for smallmouth into smaller pieces about 2 inches long and ¼ inch wide. Punch a hole in one end of each piece with an awl; the rind may be too tough to penetrate with a hook.

POPULAR STYLES of pork rind for smallmouth fishing include: (1) plain eel, (2) split-tail eel, (3) twister-tail eel and (4) pork frog. Some anglers prefer (5) plastic pork-rind imitations.

HEAT the collar of an unpainted jig head before sliding on a plastic tail. The heat melts the plastic, and when it cools and hardens, it adheres to the lead. This prevents the tail from slipping back off the collar when a fish grabs it, or when you set the hook hard and miss. Hold a lighter or match under the collar for several seconds (left), then push a plastic body over the collar (right) and allow the jig head to cool.

ADD a pre-tied stinger to your jig if smallmouth are striking short. Slip the loop onto the jig hook, then push one point of the treble into the minnow.

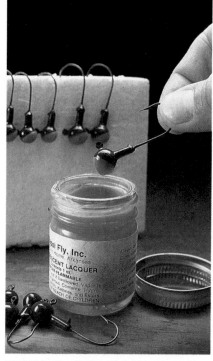

USE bicolor jig heads to increase your odds of offering the right color. You can buy them or make your own by dipping heads in fluorescent paint.

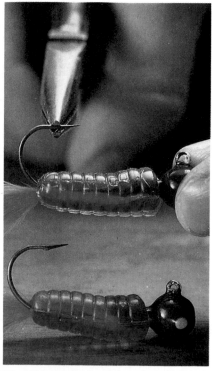

FLATTEN the barb on your jig hook if you plan on releasing your small-mouth. Or, you can remove the barb with a hook file.

Fishing with Jigging Lures

When smallmouth are tightly schooled in deep water, a jigging lure is an excellent choice. You can hold your boat directly over the school and vertically jig so the lure is continually in the fish zone. And the constant jigging motion may irritate an uninterested smallmouth into striking.

Any jigging lure will catch smallmouth, but each type has its advantages and disadvantages.

Tailspins work well in water with few obstructions. The spinner blade on the tail turns as the lure is pulled forward and helicopters as it sinks. Helicoptering slows the sink rate, giving the fish extra time to strike. But tailspins are prone to snagging, so they are not a good choice in heavy cover.

The heavy lead body of a tailspin is ideal for long-distance casting. In clear water, for instance, you can cast to distant objects, yet keep your boat far enough away that you do not spook the fish. Retrieve the tailspin using the helicoptering technique shown on the opposite page.

Vibrating blades are a good choice in murky water, but they also work well in clear water. The rapid wiggling action produces intense vibrations that smallmouth can easily detect with their lateral line. Most vibrating blades have two or more holes on the back for attaching a round-nosed snap. Placing the snap in the front hole results in a tight wiggle; the rear hole, a looser wobble. Like tailspins, vibrating blades are prone to snagging in heavy cover.

Although vibrating blades are most commonly used for vertical jigging, you can also use them for casting or trolling, much the way you would use a crankbait.

Jigging spoons have an attractive fluttering action when they sink. To a smallmouth, the action probably resembles that of an injured minnow. Jigging spoons are effective in heavy cover, like flooded timber or brush. If you get snagged, twitch the rod tip to make the spoon dance up and down. The long, heavy body swings downward with enough force to free the hook from the snag.

KEEP your line tight as a jigging lure sinks, but not too tight. If the line goes slack, a smallmouth may grab the lure and eject it without your realizing you had a strike. If you keep too much tension on the line, the lure will lose its spinning or fluttering action because it cannot sink freely. To maintain the right tension, lower your rod tip at the same rate the lure sinks, watching for the line to twitch or suddenly go slack.

But the long, heavy body can be a problem when playing a smallmouth. If the fish jumps and shakes its head, it can easily throw the spoon. If you keep a tight line, however, the chances it will throw the spoon are greatly reduced.

Jigging lures commonly used for ice fishing will also catch smallmouth during the open-water season. A lead-bodied jigging minnow works especially well because it darts to the side when jigged vertically, covering more water than most other jigging lures.

The principles of fishing with a jigging lure are much the same as with a lead-head jig. Because smallmouth generally strike as the lure is sinking, you must keep enough tension on your line that the impulse of the strike telegraphs to your rod.

For ¼- to ⅝-ounce jigging lures, use 8- to 10-pound mono. For lures over ⅝ ounce, use 12- to 14-pound mono. Most anglers prefer a stiff 6- to 7-foot bait-casting rod. This type of rod works especially well for jigging vertically. You can snap the lure sharply, and if you drift into shallower water and develop slack line, the length still gives you enough sweep to set the hook.

JIGGING LURES include: (1) tailspin, which should be tied directly to the line; (2) jigging spoon, attached with split-ring or snap-swivel; (3) vibrating blade, attached with cross-lock snap; and (4) jigging minnow, tied directly to the line or attached with cross-lock snap.

LINE UP casting targets so you can work two or more with one cast. To work a tree line with a tailspin, cast beyond one tree, reel up to it, and let the lure helicopter alongside. Then, reel to another tree and repeat.

AVOID attaching a vibrating blade with a snap-swivel. When you jig, the hooks will tangle in the swivel and ruin the lure's action. If you attach the blade with a plain round-nosed snap, the hooks will not tangle.

Fishing with Plugs

Even though a smallmouth can throw a plug more easily than most other lures, plugs account for a surprising number of trophy-class smallmouth, including the current world record.

Experienced smallmouth fishermen prefer small plugs, generally 2 to 3 inches in length. Some anglers use plugs up to 6 inches long when fishing for big smallmouth, but a plug that long greatly reduces the number of strikes.

The best type of plug to use for smallmouth depends on the season, time of day, water and weather conditions, and mood of the fish. Effective types include surface plugs such as propbaits, stickbaits, chuggers and crawlers; and subsurface plugs such as minnow plugs, crankbaits and vibrating plugs.

SURFACE PLUGS. These plugs work best when smallmouth are in the shallows. They are most effective during the spawning period or at water temperatures above 60°F. They do not work well in rough water. The best times to catch smallmouth on surface plugs are early morning, around dusk or after dark.

In general, the best surface plugs for smallmouth are those which create the least surface disturbance. Smallmouth differ from largemouth in that they will not tolerate as much commotion.

Propbaits are probably the best all-around surface plugs for smallmouth. Use a twitch-and-pause retrieve, moving your plug just enough to make the blades spin. When smallmouth are spooky or not in the mood to feed, long pauses usually draw more strikes than short ones. Some fishermen wait as long as a minute between twitches. A steady retrieve seldom works for smallmouth.

Make sure your propbait is properly tuned by blowing on the blades. If they do not spin freely, bend them until they do.

Stickbaits are more difficult to use than propbaits, but they work better over deep water. If the water is clear, they may draw smallmouth from depths as great as 20 feet. When retrieved with short, sharp jerks, a stickbait dances enticingly from side to side, mimicking an injured minnow.

Chuggers are used mainly for largemouth, but they will catch smallmouth if worked properly. The most common mistake is to twitch the chugger too hard, causing a big splash and spooking the fish. Instead, work it with short, gentle twitches followed by pauses. Chuggers do not work well in current because they dig too much water.

Crawlers create a lot of surface disturbance and do not work as well as other surface lures during daylight hours. But they can be effective at night, when smallmouth are more aggressive and less easily spooked. Normally, crawlers are retrieved steadily so they produce a gurgling sound, but for smallmouth a reel-and-pause retrieve often works better.

Surface plugs should be tied directly to the line. A snap-swivel or steel leader may weight down the nose of the plug so it catches too much water when retrieved. A 5½- to 6-foot medium-power spinning or baitcasting outfit with 6- to 10-pound mono is adequate for most surface plugs.

SUBSURFACE PLUGS. These plugs will catch smallmouth under a much wider variety of conditions than surface plugs. They work well in rough water and at water temperatures as low as 50°F. Subsurface plugs can be fished by trolling as well as casting, and at any depth where smallmouth are likely to be found.

Minnow plugs come in floating and sinking models, but floaters seem to work best for smallmouth. Most floaters have short lips and run at depths of 5 feet or less. But long-lipped floaters run as deep as 12 feet.

When smallmouth are in very shallow water, twitch a short-lipped floater so it darts just beneath the surface then floats back up. Pause occasionally between twitches as you would with a surface plug. A hungry smallmouth finds this erratic retrieve difficult to resist.

In deeper water, use a steady retrieve with a periodic twitch to change the action. By attaching your minnow plug to a three-way swivel rig (page 145) or adding a pinch-on sinker to your line, you can easily reach depths of 20 feet or more.

Minnow plugs are light for their size, so they are difficult to cast. To make casting easier, use 4- to

6-pound mono and a spinning rod with a light tip. To avoid dampening the plug's action, attach it with a loop knot or small, round-nosed snap, or position your knot on the lower part of the attachment eye as described on page 103.

Crankbaits come in shallow- and deep-running models. Shallow runners have small, sharply sloping lips and track at 6 feet or less. Deep runners have lips that do not slope as sharply. They track as deep as 12 feet. Some extra-deep runners track as deep as 18 feet and reach depths of 25 feet when trolled.

Crankbaits can be cast a long distance and retrieved rapidly, so they will cover a lot of water. The large lip tends to deflect off obstructions, keeping the hooks from snagging. Because of their snag resistance, crankbaits are ideal for working the rocky

shorelines and reefs where smallmouth are commonly found.

In cold water or whenever smallmouth are not in the mood to feed, a slow, stop-and-go retrieve is more effective than a fast, steady retrieve. But in warm water, the reverse is sometimes true.

Trolling a deep-running crankbait along a breakline or over a deep reef is an excellent technique for locating smallmouth. If you find a school of smallmouth but they quit biting, you can switch to a slower method like jig or live-bait fishing.

Whether you are casting over a 5-foot flat with a shallow-running crankbait or trolling a 15-foot reef with a deep runner, try to keep the crankbait's lip digging bottom or bumping obstructions. The interruption in the action triggers more strikes.

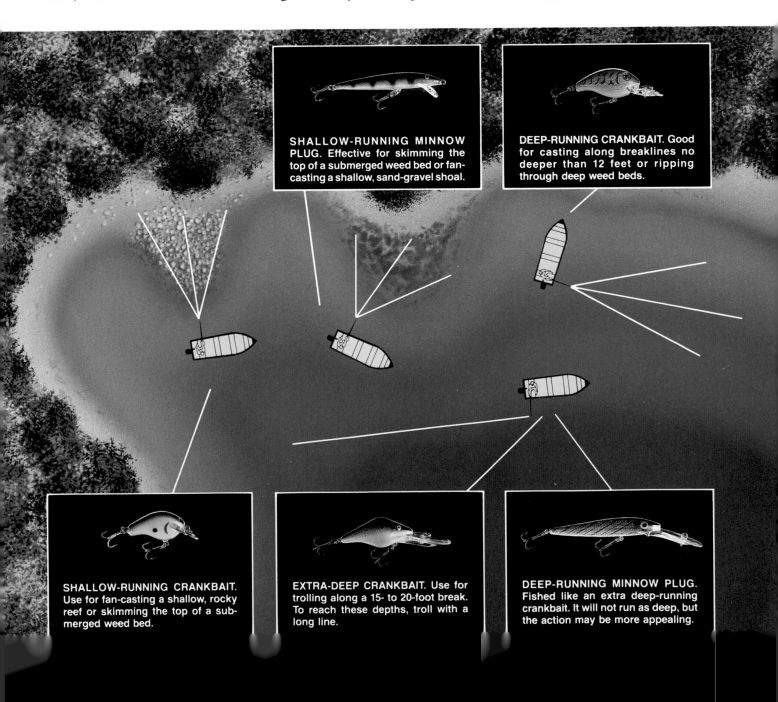

SHALLOW-RUNNING MINNOW PLUG. Effective for skimming the top of a submerged weed bed or fan-casting a shallow, sand-gravel shoal.

DEEP-RUNNING CRANKBAIT. Good for casting along breaklines no deeper than 12 feet or ripping through deep weed beds.

SHALLOW-RUNNING CRANKBAIT. Use for fan-casting a shallow, rocky reef or skimming the top of a submerged weed bed.

EXTRA-DEEP CRANKBAIT. Use for trolling along a 15- to 20-foot break. To reach these depths, troll with a long line.

DEEP-RUNNING MINNOW PLUG. Fished like an extra deep-running crankbait. It will not run as deep, but the action may be more appealing.

Deep-running crankbaits have a lot of water resistance, so most veteran anglers prefer medium-power baitcasting or spinning gear with 8- to 14-pound mono. For most shallow runners, light- to medium-power spinning gear with 6- to 10-pound mono is adequate. If your crankbait comes with a split-ring or snap, tie your line directly to it. If not, attach the lure with a small, round-nosed snap or a loop knot.

Minnow plugs and crankbaits must be properly tuned for peak performance. If the plug veers to the side, it is out of tune. To make it run straight, bend or turn the attachment eye in the direction opposite the way the plug is veering.

Vibrating plugs have a tight wiggle that appeals to smallmouth. They work best when retrieved at medium to high speed.

The vibrating action makes them especially effective in murky water. Models with beads or shot inside a rattle chamber create even more vibration and noise. But vibrating plugs do not have lips, so they snag more easily than crankbaits.

You can fish vibrating plugs at practically any depth. To fish in the shallows, begin your retrieve as soon as the plug hits the water. To fish in deeper water, feed enough line to let the plug reach bottom before beginning your retrieve. Keep the lure near bottom by pausing occasionally to let it sink.

Vibrating plugs, especially those with lead shot, are easy to cast. A medium-power spinning or baitcasting outfit with 6- to 10-pound mono works well in most situations. Attach a vibrating plug the same way as a crankbait.

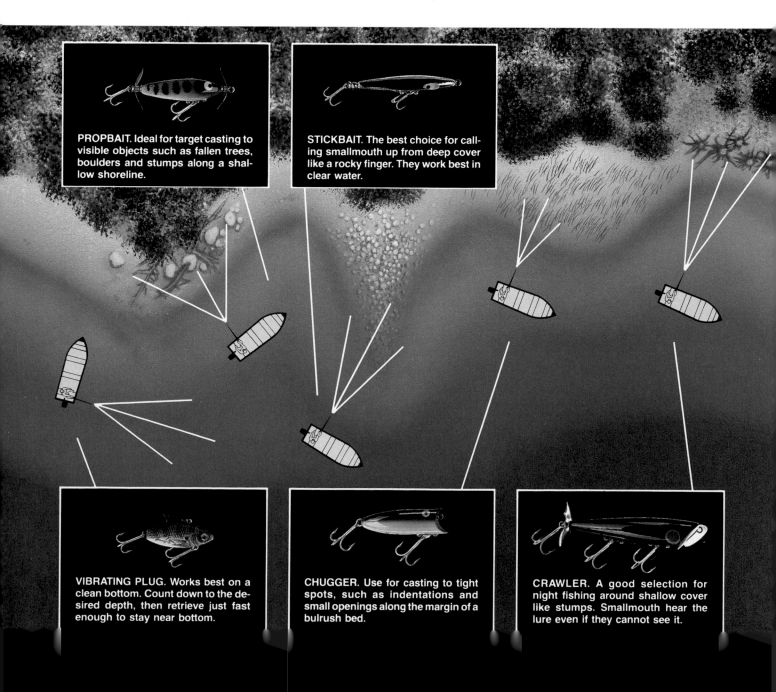

PROPBAIT. Ideal for target casting to visible objects such as fallen trees, boulders and stumps along a shallow shoreline.

STICKBAIT. The best choice for calling smallmouth up from deep cover like a rocky finger. They work best in clear water.

VIBRATING PLUG. Works best on a clean bottom. Count down to the desired depth, then retrieve just fast enough to stay near bottom.

CHUGGER. Use for casting to tight spots, such as indentations and small openings along the margin of a bulrush bed.

CRAWLER. A good selection for night fishing around shallow cover like stumps. Smallmouth hear the lure even if they cannot see it.

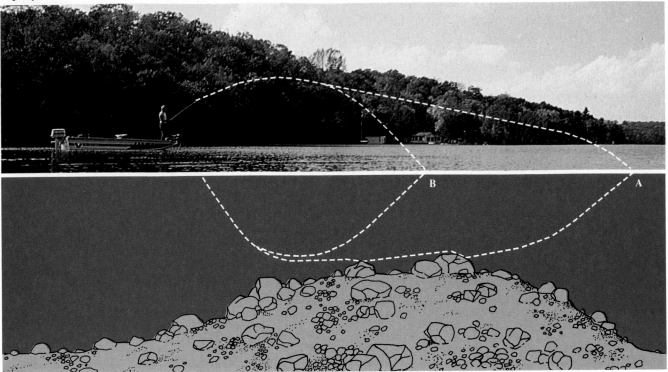

CAST a crankbait well past the area you want to fish. This way, it will dive to the necessary depth before reaching the fish zone. When fishing a submerged reef, for instance, cast your crankbait to point A, which is far enough beyond the reef so that the plug will tick the top of the reef. If you cast to point B, which is directly over the reef, the plug will be well past the reef by the time it dives deep enough.

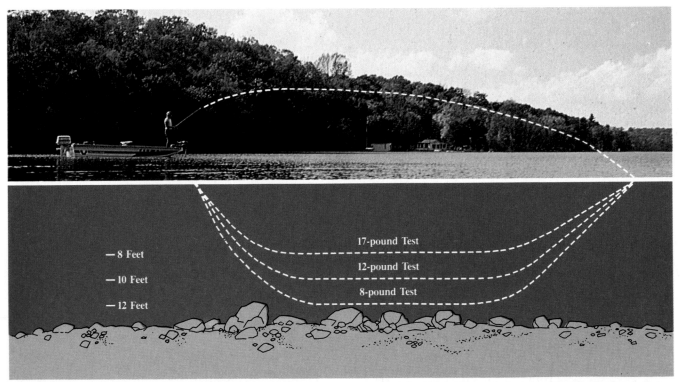

USE lighter line to make your crankbait run deeper. Smaller diameter line has less water resistance, so there is less drag to force your plug upward. And you can cast farther, so the plug has more time to reach its depth potential. With 17-pound mono (top), a deep-diving crankbait will run at only about 8 feet. With 12-pound mono (middle), it would run at about 10 feet. With 8-pound mono (bottom) it would dive to about 12 feet.

How to Attach a Minnow Plug for Maximum Action

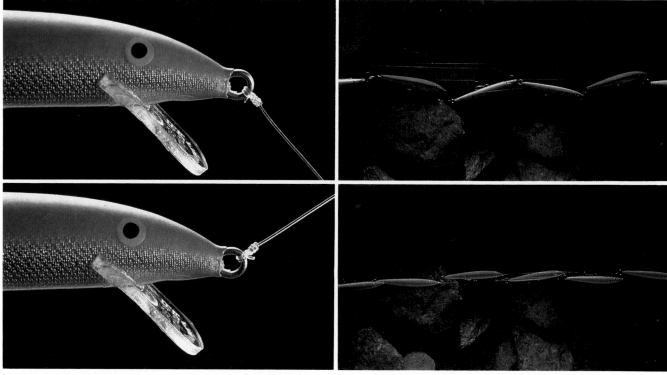

MULTIPLE EXPOSURE PHOTOGRAPH

TIE on a minnow plug with a knot that clinches tightly to the attachment eye. Slide the knot toward the bottom of the eye (top) for the most wiggle. If you get snagged or catch a fish, the knot may slip toward the top of the eye

(bottom) and the action will diminish. Before you resume fishing, slide the knot back to the bottom. To minimize the slippage problem, use a knot that has two loops of line through the eye.

CAST a propbait or crawler onto the shoreline, then pull it back into the water. Smallmouth are accustomed to feeding on prey that hops into the water, so they may mistake the plug for a frog or large insect.

PAUSE several seconds after casting a crankbait or minnow plug into the shallows before starting to retrieve. The splash may draw a smallmouth's attention, and when it swims in to investigate, it spots the floating plug.

Fishing with Spinners

Smallmouth are quick to notice any unusual flash or vibration. Spinners produce a good deal of both, explaining why they are so effective.

Spinners commonly used for smallmouth fishing include spinnerbaits, standard spinners, weight-forward spinners and buzzbaits.

SPINNERBAITS. A spinnerbait is a good choice when smallmouth are in heavy cover. Its safety-pin design makes it relatively snagless. It can be fished in shallow or deep water, and is one of the best lures for night fishing.

Smallmouth prefer spinnerbaits smaller than the ones normally used for largemouth. Most small-mouth anglers use $\frac{1}{8}$- to $\frac{1}{4}$-ounce models, but some use panfish models weighing as little as $\frac{1}{32}$ ounce. Spinnerbaits are usually fished without live bait or other attractors, although some fishermen add pork trailers or twister tails to reduce the sink rate.

To fish a spinnerbait in shallow water, cast well past an obstruction like a boulder or stump, then reel steadily. Keep your rod tip high so the spinner

blades bulge the surface. Try to make the lure bump the obstruction. The change in action often triggers a strike.

In deeper water, let the spinnerbait helicopter to bottom, reel a short distance, then let it helicopter to bottom again. Using this technique, you can *walk* it down a drop-off or keep it at a constant depth.

For night fishing, use a fairly large spinnerbait, from ¼ to ½ ounce. A large blade sends out more vibrations than a small one, making it easier for smallmouth to find the lure. And smallmouth seem more aggressive at night, so the large size does not discourage strikes. Large spinnerbaits also work well during the nesting period and in late fall, when smallmouth begin their pre-winter feeding spree.

A medium-power spinning outfit with 6- to 8-pound mono works best for fishing small spinnerbaits. But a medium to medium-heavy power baitcasting outfit with 12- to 20-pound mono is better suited to heavy spinnerbaits or to fishing in dense cover.

STANDARD SPINNERS. A favorite of many old-timers, the standard spinner is not as widely used for smallmouth as it once was. Nevertheless, it is still an excellent smallmouth lure. Its decline in popularity is probably due to the increasing popularity of other smallmouth lures, like crankbaits.

Standard spinners work best in shallow water, especially for casting to rocks, stumps and other visible cover. Simply toss the spinner a little past your target, then retrieve steadily, just fast enough to

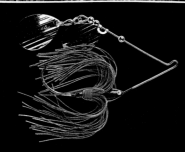

TANDEM SPINNERBAIT. The lift from the extra blade allows you to retrieve slowly through shallow cover like a bulrush bed.

BUZZBAIT. A good choice for casting over shallow weeds or brush. Can also be used for calling smallmouth up from deep water.

SINGLE-SPIN SPINNERBAIT. Short-armed models work well for helicoptering down a drop-off or alongside cover like a weedbed or stump.

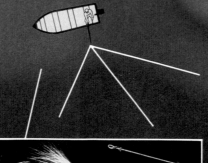

WEIGHT-FORWARD SPINNER. Ideal for casting along breaklines, and around reefs, points and other deep-water structure.

STANDARD SPINNER. Use for working shallow structure with few snags, or the edges of fallen trees or other snaggy cover.

make the blade turn. To make the spinner run a little deeper, attach split-shot to your line about a foot ahead of the lure.

A spinner with a blade no larger than size 3 works best. Some fishermen tip their hook with a leech, a piece of nightcrawler or a small minnow.

For maximum sport, use an ultralight spinning rod with 4- to 6-pound mono. To avoid line twist, attach the spinner with a ball-bearing swivel.

WEIGHT-FORWARD SPINNERS. These lures work better than standard spinners in deep water or current. They sink faster than other types of spinners, and hold their depth well.

Weight-forward spinners are normally tipped with some type of live bait, usually a minnow, leech or piece of nightcrawler. But tipping is not always a good idea. If smallmouth are striking short, you may hook more of them by removing the bait.

To fish a weight-forward spinner, make a long cast, then keep your line taut as the lure sinks. The blade turns as the lure drops, so smallmouth may strike before it hits bottom. When you feel bottom, lift the lure a foot or so with an upward sweep of your rod, then begin your retrieve. Reel just fast enough to keep the lure near bottom, occasionally sweeping the rod to change the spinner's action.

When fishing over a snaggy bottom, count the lure down to the right depth rather than letting it sink to bottom and snag.

Weight-forward spinners used for smallmouth range from ¼ to ½ ounce. A medium-power spinning outfit with 6- to 8-pound mono is ideal for these lures. Weight-forward spinners will not twist your line, so you do not need a swivel.

BUZZBAITS. Like most other surface lures, buzzbaits work best when the surface is relatively calm. Although buzzbaits are normally used for catching largemouth in dense or matted weeds, they also can be effective for smallmouth in some situations.

At night, when smallmouth may have trouble seeing a lure, they cannot help but notice a buzzbait's noisy, sputtering action. Buzzbaits also work well in early morning and around dusk, when smallmouth are feeding in the shallows. Although they are normally fished over depths of 10 feet or less, there are times when they will draw smallmouth from depths as great as 20 feet, particularly in clear water. A spinnerbait buzzed across the surface will also draw smallmouth from deep water.

Smallmouth prefer buzzbaits ranging in size from ¼ to ½ ounce. Use the same tackle you would when fishing with spinnerbaits.

Tips for Fishing with Spinners

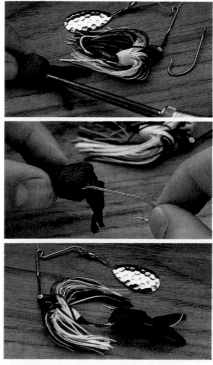

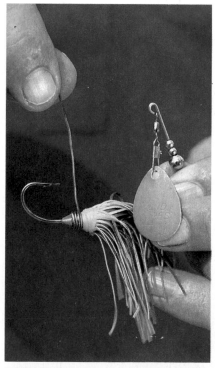

MAKE a trailer-hook attractor by punching a hole in a pork chunk (top), inserting a trailer (middle) and forcing the main hook through the pork and the trailer eye (bottom).

WRAP thin-diameter lead solder around the body of your spinner to increase its weight without increasing its size. With the extra weight, the lure casts easier and runs deeper.

ADD an extra blade to a spinnerbait to increase its lift so you can retrieve more slowly. Attach a swivel to the extra blade and clip it to the snap-swivel on the main blade.

Fly Fishing for Smallmouth

Anyone who has battled a big smallmouth on a fly rod would be quick to agree that few other types of fishing are as exciting. When a smallmouth smashes a fly and catapults into the air, even an experienced angler has a tough time maintaining his composure.

Not only is fly fishing for smallmouth a lot of fun, it is extremely effective. Flies imitate natural small-mouth foods more closely than most other lures. The most popular smallmouth flies are subsurface types including streamers, crayfish and leech imitations, and nymphs; and surface types including bugs and dry flies.

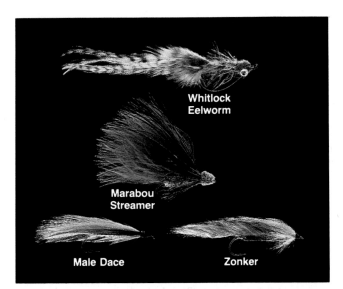

STREAMERS. The elongated shape of a streamer usually imitates that of a baitfish. Among the top streamers for smallmouth are jigging flies. They work better than other types of streamers in still water, because the weighted head makes them move with an appealing up-and-down action; in addition, they work well in current. Marabou streamers also are effective in still or moving water. They have a long, flowing wing that gives them an attractive breathing action. Hackle-wing and buck-tail streamers are most effective in current; they lack sufficient action in still water.

Many streamer patterns are tied in both weighted and unweighted versions. A few have monofilament weedguards. Streamers in sizes 2 to 6 are most popular for smallmouth fishing.

When fishing a streamer in current, quarter your cast upstream, then let the streamer sink and drift naturally until it swings below you. If a curve or *belly* forms in your line during the drift, use your rod tip to *mend* the line. Flip the line into the air and straighten it without lifting the fly from the water.

When the fly has swung below you, retrieve it with short jerks to imitate a minnow struggling against the current. Strikes may come at any time during the drift or retrieve.

Cast well upstream of cover like a boulder or log, so the streamer will have time to sink before reaching it. An unweighted streamer fished on a floating line is the best choice where the current and depth are moderate. Use a weighted streamer or a sink-tip line in deeper or faster water.

In long, still pools or in lakes, cast around likely cover, let the streamer sink and then retrieve it with foot-long pulls to imitate a darting baitfish. At times, a steady retrieve or a series of short twitches may work better.

For fishing in still water at depths less than 5 feet, a floating line is usually best. For depths from 5 to 10 feet, switch to a sink-tip line. For greater depths, you will need a sinking line.

Streamer fishing requires the same basic equipment used for most other types of fly fishing. In streams, most fishermen prefer 6- or 7-weight rods and lines; in lakes, 7- or 8-weight. All lines should be weight-forward tapers. With floating lines, use 7½- to 9-foot leaders; with sink-tip or sinking lines, 3- to 4-foot leaders. Leader tippets range from 6- to 12-pound test, depending on the size of the fly and the type of cover. For maximum action, attach your fly with a loop knot.

Schley Crayfish

Dave's Softshell Crayfish

Wooly Leech

Lectric Leech

CRAYFISH AND LEECH FLIES. These flies mimic some of the smallmouth's favorite foods. Crayfish flies have realistic claws made of hair or feathers. Leech flies have a long tail made from marabou or a strip of chamois. Marabou leech patterns in dark brown or black also make excellent

hellgrammite imitations. Many crayfish and leech flies are weighted, and some have mono weed-guards. Sizes 2 to 6 work best for smallmouth.

Drift a crayfish fly in current much as you would a streamer. When the drift is complete, crawl the fly back along the bottom, or swim it just above bottom with a series of short pulls. Crayfish flies that sink rapidly can be fished in current with a floating line; those that sink slowly require a sink-tip line.

In lakes, crayfish flies take smallmouth on rocky points, reefs, ledges and other places where crayfish are found. Make the longest cast you can, let the fly sink to bottom, then retrieve it slowly with short pulls. Choose your line according to depth, as you would in lake fishing with streamers.

Crayfish and leech flies require the same basic fly-fishing equipment used with streamers.

Dave's Dragon Nymph

Prince Hellgrammite

Casual Dress Nymph

Damselfly Nymph

NYMPHS. Big nymphs rank among the top lures for river smallmouth. They also work well in lakes. Nymphs resemble immature forms of aquatic insects, an important part of the smallmouth's diet. They are effective whether or not a hatch is in progress. Nymphs that imitate hellgrammites or the larvae of dragonflies and damselflies are most popular for smallmouth. Sizes 6 to 10 work best.

Different types of aquatic insects move through the water in different ways, so you can use a wide variety of presentations when fishing nymphs. You can let them drift with the current, or retrieve them with long, slow pulls or gentle twitches followed by pauses. A weighted nymph sometimes works best if you let the current roll it along bottom, like an immature insect tumbling or crawling over the rocks.

Strikes may be hard to detect when fishing with nymphs. Sometimes a smallmouth swims up and simply closes its mouth on the nymph. Anytime you feel a tick or notice the tip of your line twitch or stop moving, set the hook.

Nymph fishing is done with the same basic tackle used for streamer fishing.

BUGS. Sometimes called bass bugs, these floating flies generally work best in early morning and around dusk, when smallmouth are feeding in the shallows. They are most effective in calm water.

Bugs have bodies of hard cork or plastic, or of clipped deer or elk hair. Hard-bodied bugs are more durable, but hair bugs feel more like real food. A smallmouth will hold a hair bug slightly longer, giving you an extra instant to set the hook.

Before you fish a hair bug, treat it with a paste-type floatant. If it starts to sink, dry it with a powdered dessicant and then reapply the floatant.

Smallmouth prefer bugs in sizes 1 to 6. For fishing in heavy cover, select a bug with a monofilament weedguard. Bugs have a lot of wind resistance, so they require a heavy rod and line, usually 7 to 8 weight. Your rod should be 8 to 9 feet long. Use a bug-taper line, which will lay a bug out faster and easier than an ordinary weight-forward line.

The following types of bugs work best for smallmouth fishing:

Poppers — The cupped or flattened face produces a popping or gurgling sound. Most poppers imitate frogs, mice or insects. Many have rubber legs, which give them a remarkably lifelike look.

Most poppers are designed for still water. The face will dig into a current, creating too much disturbance and making it difficult to lift the popper off the water for a new cast.

In most cases, the best retrieve consists of slight twitches that produce only moderate pops or no pops at all. Pause a few seconds between twitches. If you jerk the popper too hard, you will pull it away from the cover too soon, and the loud popping may spook the fish. If a twitch-and-pause retrieve does not produce, try twitching the popper more rapidly with no pauses.

Pencil poppers, which are long and very thin, should be fished with a darting retrieve to imitate an injured minnow. Because of their slender shape, they work as well in current as in still water.

How to Handle Fly Tackle for Smallmouth

CAST the fly just to the side of a log, brush pile, rock, or other cover likely to hold a smallmouth. Aim the cast parallel to the water, or slightly below parallel. If you aim the cast too high, the line and leader will be slack when they settle on the water.

LOWER your rod tip close to the water as the last few feet of line shoot to the target and unroll. The rod, line and leader should point directly at the target, with no slack. This way, you can set the hook instantly should a bass strike when the fly hits the water.

Sliders — Designed to imitate a minnow struggling on the surface, these flies have a bullet-shaped body which makes them easier to cast than a popper.

Sliders do not create as much surface disturbance as poppers, so they sometimes work better when smallmouth are spooky. They do not dig like a popper, so you can fish them in current or still water.

You can retrieve sliders with a twitch-and-pause technique or a slow, steady pull. Occasionally, smallmouth prefer them skittering across the surface and kicking up spray.

Divers — The head design causes these flies to dive when pulled forward, much like a frog. Most have a long wing made of feathers or a fur strip. Divers work well in either still or moving water.

When retrieved with a short pull followed by a pause, a diver plunges beneath the surface, emitting a stream of air bubbles, then floats back up. If you strip in line rapidly without pausing, a diver will stay underwater. And when fished with gentle twitches and pauses, it reacts much like a slider.

Because of its surface and subsurface action, a diver will often take smallmouth when other types of bass bugs fail.

Other bugs — A wide variety of bugs are shaped like frogs, moths, mice, dragonflies or other smallmouth foods. Generally, they have less action than other types of bugs. As a result, they cannot attract fish from much distance. They work best when cast precisely to a rise or to shallow cover. These bugs are normally retrieved slowly, with slight twitches followed by long pauses.

Badger Bivisible

Grizzly Wulff

Sofa Pillow

Goofus Bug

DRY FLIES. A dry fly can be identified by its prominent hackle collar, which helps keep it afloat. Although dry flies are not as popular for smallmouth as bugs, they sometimes work very well in rivers, especially when a hatch of large mayflies or stoneflies is in progress. Under these conditions, dry flies in sizes 4 to 6 are the best choices.

The most productive way to work a dry fly for smallmouth is to angle your cast downstream, allow the fly to drift over a likely spot, then skate it there by holding your rod tip high. Smallmouth nearly always prefer the skating action to a dead drift.

Like hair bugs, dry flies should be treated with a floatant before fishing. Paste floatants last longer than liquid types and should be applied sparingly with the fingertips.

For skating a dry fly, use a 9- to 9½-foot rod matched to a 6-weight floating line, and a 9- to 12-foot leader with a 7- to 10-pound tippet.

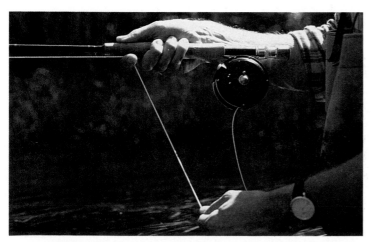

HOLD the line against the rod handle with the forefinger of your right hand. Strip in line with your left hand, letting it slip beneath your finger. Between pulls, pinch the line securely against the handle in case a fish should strike. Keep your rod tip low throughout the retrieve.

SET THE HOOK by sharply lifting the rod with a stiff wrist. At the same time, pull the line down with your left hand. Keep the rod nearly parallel to the water; raising the tip high would not increase your hooking power and could tangle the line on the rod if you miss the fish.

Fishing with Soft Plastics

Modern soft-plastic baits appeal to smallmouth because of their natural look and lifelike texture. Soft-plastic worms, salamanders, lizards, crayfish and frogs in 3- to 4-inch sizes are more effective than the larger soft plastics used for largemouth.

You can rig soft plastics *Texas style* (opposite page) for fishing in weeds, brush or other dense cover. Or, you can rig them with an exposed hook for fishing on a clean bottom. Your hooking percentage will be higher with the hook exposed.

Soft plastics are normally weighted with a cone sinker or split-shot, or with an egg sinker rigged to slip. They can also be fished on a jig head, either with the hook exposed or buried in the plastic. Some jig heads, such as the *keeper* style (opposite page), are designed specifically for soft plastics.

Normally, soft plastics are retrieved with a jigging action, much as you would retrieve a lead-head jig. Smallmouth usually grab the lure as it sinks, so you must keep your line taut to detect a strike. But when smallmouth are not feeding, you may have better success by simply crawling the lure on the bottom. This *do-nuthin'* retrieve works best with a 3½- to 4-inch plastic worm rigged with two exposed hooks.

When fishing soft plastics rigged Texas style, use a medium- to heavy-power baitcasting outfit with 12- to 14-pound mono. You need a fairly stiff rod to drive the hook through the soft plastic and into the fish's mouth. A medium-power spinning outfit with 6- to 8-pound mono works better when using soft plastics with exposed hooks.

TREAT your soft plastics with worm oil to keep them soft and pliable. Store them in a zip-lock bag; if you store them in a tackle box, they may get wet and their colors may turn milky. Do not mix different colors in the same bag. In time, the colors will bleed together.

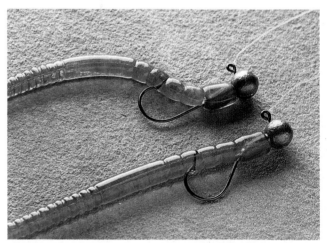

BEND your jig hook when you intend to bury it in a soft-plastic lure. If not bent (top), the hook penetrates the worm at an extreme angle, causing missed strikes. With the hook bent (bottom), the point will come through straighter so you are more likely to hook the fish.

SMALLMOUTH take most types of live bait by inhaling them along with a volume of water. This photograph shows a smallmouth sucking a minnow into its mouth and expelling the excess water through its gills. The slight tap that you often feel when a smallmouth picks up your bait results from this sharp suction.

KEEPER JIG. Rig with a plastic crayfish for fishing rocky structure. Insert the barbed shaft into the tail and run the hook out the back.

WORM HOOK WITH NO SINKER. Used for fishing worms or other soft plastics over shallow weeds or brush. Bury the hook point.

TEXAS RIG. Suited to fishing in deeper weeds or brush, or in any heavy cover. Bury the hook point, add a cone sinker, and peg it so it cannot slide away from the hook.

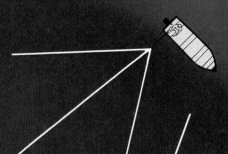

DO-NUTHIN' RIG. A good choice for fishing deep water with a clean bottom. Add a barrel swivel and egg sinker 2 to 3 feet ahead of the worm.

WEEDLESS HOOK. The best rig for fishing plastic frogs and lizards in heavy cover. A foot ahead, add enough split-shot to reach the desired depth.

Fishing with Live Bait

Finding good live bait for smallmouth can be difficult. Bait shops may not carry shiners, soft-shelled crayfish, hellgrammites or other effective baits, so you may have to catch your own. But the effort is well worth it because there are many situations in which these live baits will outfish artificial lures by a wide margin.

When the water temperature is below 50°F, live bait presented very slowly is often the best choice for smallmouth. With their metabolic rate slowed by the cold water, they are not likely to chase a fast-moving lure.

Live bait is also the best choice when weather changes, like cold fronts, slow feeding activity. In low-competition waters (pages 30-31), smallmouth inspect their food closely before striking, so there is no substitute for real food.

But there are disadvantages to live-bait fishing. In most cases, strikes are more difficult to detect. A smallmouth does not always attack the bait with a slashing strike; more often, it simply inhales the bait and swims away slowly. Detecting this subtle pick-up requires a good sense of feel that must be developed through experience.

Another disadvantage of live bait is that you cannot cover as much area as you could with an artificial. With a crankbait, for instance, you can fan-cast a fair-sized reef in just a few minutes and catch any active smallmouth. Covering the same area with live bait might take an hour or more.

Smallmouth will take a wide variety of live baits, including minnows and other baitfish, crayfish, nightcrawlers, leeches, waterdogs, spring lizards, frogs, hellgrammites, grasshoppers and crickets.

MINNOWS AND OTHER BAITFISH. During most of the year, 2- to 3-inch minnows work best, but in late fall, some fishermen use minnows as long as 6 inches.

Shiners rank among the top smallmouth baits, but they may be difficult to keep alive, especially in summer. If you bought your shiners from a bait shop where they were held in cold water, you will have to keep them in cold water. Check the water temperature, add ice when necessary and keep your minnow bucket inside a cooler. Shiners held in water this cold will probably die within a few minutes when fished in warm water, so you will have to change your bait frequently.

If you catch your own shiners or buy shiners held at lake temperature, you can keep them alive in a well-aerated cooler or garbage can. About every half hour, add some fresh lake water.

Common shiners and golden shiners are not as difficult to keep alive as other types of shiners and generally do not require cold water.

Fatheads, also called tuffies or mudminnows, are much hardier than shiners and are easy to keep alive in even the hottest weather. However, they are much less effective than shiners.

Redtail chubs and creek chubs are not as hardy as fatheads, but hardier than shiners. Their large size makes them a good choice in late fall.

Other baitfish used for smallmouth include shad; dace; mummichogs, popular mainly in the East; madtoms or willow cats, favorites in big rivers; eels, an extremely hardy and effective bait popular along the West Coast; and practically any other type of small fish commonly found in local waters, including immature lampreys.

CRAYFISH. In many waters, crayfish make up the bulk of the smallmouth's diet, so it is not surprising that they are an excellent smallmouth bait, particularly in summer.

Soft-shelled crayfish, or *soft craws,* work better than the hard-shelled type. But smallmouth eat plenty of hard-shells, so there is no reason to avoid using them for bait.

Do not use crayfish longer than 3 inches unless you are fishing for big smallmouth. An average-sized smallmouth will take a larger one, but you will have trouble setting the hook.

While fishing, keep your crayfish in a flow-through style minnow bucket. For long-term storage, refrigerate them in a container with damp sphagnum moss or layers of wet newspaper.

NIGHTCRAWLERS. Although crawlers are mainly a warm-weather bait, they will catch smallmouth well into the fall.

To insure that your crawlers stay lively, keep them in a large styrofoam container or a cooler. On a hot day, they will die in an hour or less if left in the sun. You can keep crawlers for months if you store them in a refrigerator in a box of worm bedding or moss.

Nightcrawlers work best when allowed to trail from a moving bait rig. They are less effective when gobbed onto the hook. When using a large crawler, you will increase your hooking percentage if you break it into two pieces.

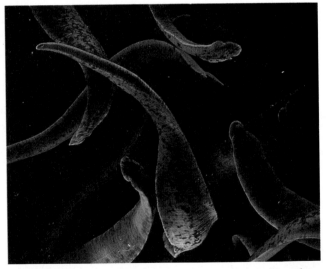

LEECHES. The undulating action of a leech makes it one of the most effective smallmouth baits. Like crawlers, leeches work best in warm weather. If the water temperature is below 50°F, they curl into a tight ball.

Only one species, the ribbon leech, is known to be a good smallmouth bait. You can buy ribbon leeches in most bait shops throughout the north-central states. Their popularity is slowly spreading, but you may have difficulty finding them in other areas.

Smallmouth prefer leeches measuring 3 to 4 inches when stretched out, but some trophy specialists use jumbo leeches measuring 6 inches or more.

SPRING LIZARDS. These slender salamanders are a popular smallmouth bait in the Southeast, but they are rarely used in other parts of the country.

Spring lizards are used in the adult form. You can find them under damp, rotting logs or under flat, half-submerged rocks along creek margins. They will stay alive in a container filled with moist leaves or moss. Keep them cool and make sure they can get air. For long-term storage, keep them in a refrigerator at about 45°F.

WATERDOGS. Many experts rate waterdogs as the top bait for trophy smallmouth. Waterdogs range in length from 4 to 8 inches, with the 4- to 6-inch sizes being most effective. Waterdogs are generally too large for average-sized smallmouth.

Waterdogs are the larval stage of the tiger salamander. Be sure you fish with the larval form; if your salamander does not have gills, it has transformed into the adult stage which is not as effective.

Keep waterdogs in a cooler filled with water no warmer than 50°F. If you change the water once a week, they will live for months.

FROGS. Veteran river fishermen know that frogs are an excellent smallmouth bait in fall. When the fall frog migration begins, smallmouth sometimes hug the bank, waiting for an unsuspecting frog to hop in.

Frogs no more than 3 inches long work best. With bigger ones, you will have trouble hooking the fish.

One of the best ways to keep frogs is to put them in a wire-mesh box. Cut a 6-inch hole in the top and attach a piece of inner tube with a slit large enough for your hand. This way, you can grab one frog without the rest jumping out.

Keep frogs at a temperature of 70°F or less, and do not let them dehydrate.

HELLGRAMMITES.

HELLGRAMMITES. In the opinion of many accomplished smallmouth anglers, the hellgrammite, which is the larval stage of the dobsonfly, is the best bait for stream fishing. Dragonfly nymphs and other large aquatic insect larvae also make good smallmouth baits.

Like crayfish, hellgrammites are a natural smallmouth food. Most are no more than 3 inches long, so they are much easier for a smallmouth to swallow. They live under rocks in riffle areas. Bait shops rarely stock hellgrammites, but you can catch your own by turning over rocks and holding a fine-mesh net just downstream. Handle them carefully because they have strong pincers that can give you a painful nip.

You can keep a day's supply of hellgrammites in a plastic container filled with damp leaves or moss. To keep them for an extended period, put them in a large container filled with water and some type of aquatic vegetation. Keep the water cool and aerate it with an aquarium pump.

Hellgrammites are one of the toughest baits. They can be cast repeatedly without tearing off the hook and will stay alive indefinitely.

GRASSHOPPERS AND CRICKETS. These insects are usually considered to be panfish bait, but they also work well for smallmouth. They are most effective for stream fishing, especially on warm summer days when smallmouth feed heavily on floating insects.

A handy container for keeping crickets and grasshoppers is a coffee can with a plastic lid. Punch small holes in the can and lid for air, then cut a ½-inch by 1-inch tab in the lid. When you need bait, push the tab in and shake the can. This way, you do not have to open the lid and give the other insects an opportunity to escape.

For extended storage, add a damp paper towel and some cornmeal, and keep the container in a cool place. The insects will stay alive for weeks.

Live-bait Techniques for Smallmouth

How you present your bait depends mainly on the depth of the water you are fishing. When smallmouth are at depths of 10 feet or less, simply tie on a hook and pinch a split-shot or two about 18 inches up the line. In deeper water, a slip-sinker rig is a better choice. You will need more weight to reach bottom, so if your sinker is not rigged to slip, smallmouth may feel too much resistance and drop the bait.

Slip-bobber rigs work well for fishing tight schools, especially when smallmouth are not in the mood to feed. And you can set your depth so the bait rides just above rocks or other snags.

Another technique that is less popular, but very effective, is free-lining. This is the most natural of all live-bait presentations because the bait swims freely, with no drag from a sinker.

With any live-bait technique, the most important consideration is to present the bait to make it look natural. This means using as little weight as possible, small hooks, and light, low-visibility line with no heavy leader. Many live-bait specialists use clear 4-pound-test monofilament for practically all of their fishing.

A 6- to 7-foot medium-power, slow- to medium-action spinning rod is a good choice for most types of live-bait fishing. A slow-action rod reduces the odds of snapping the bait off the hook when you cast and is more forgiving should you mistakenly tighten the line when a smallmouth is biting.

Split-shot Fishing

This technique is ideal for smallmouth because they spend so much of their time in relatively shallow water. A split-shot rig takes only seconds to tie and is easy to use.

The most important consideration in using a split-shot rig is the amount of weight. Too much, and the rig will sink quickly and wedge in rocks or other snags. Too little, and a lively bait will keep it from sinking. By using just enough shot to barely sink your bait, you can swim the rig along bottom without snagging, yet the bait can move freely and keep its natural look. To use a split-shot rig properly, follow steps 1 through 5.

1. LOB-CAST a split-shot rig (inset) past the spot you want to fish, then let it sink to bottom. A sweeping sidearm motion reduces the chances of snapping the bait off the hook when you cast.

2. POINT your rod tip in the direction of the rig while reeling up any slack line. Do not begin your retrieve until you are sure all of the slack has been removed.

3. SLOWLY LIFT your rod to nearly vertical. Then lower it to horizontal, reeling to keep the line taut. Continue to lift and lower, watching the line and rod tip.

4. DROP your rod tip when you notice any twitch, sideways movement or excess drag. Point the rod at the fish and feed line when it runs with the bait. When it stops running, tighten the line until you feel resistance.

5. SET THE HOOK with a powerful snap of the wrists. For maximum hook-setting leverage, keep your elbows close to your body and pull sharply with your forearms instead of extending your arms full length.

Slip-sinker Fishing

When a smallmouth swims away with the bait, it feels no resistance because the line slides freely through the sinker.

Normally, you can use a ¼-ounce slip sinker for depths of 20 feet ot less. But you can also use a heavier one because the sinker slips on the line. The extra weight allows you to keep your line more nearly vertical, so you will feel bites more easily and get fewer snags.

You can fish a slip-sinker rig in shallow water, much like a split-shot rig. But slip-sinker rigs are usually trolled along a breakline. You can cover a lot of water and easily fish as deep as 40 feet.

Most fishermen backtroll when using a slip-sinker rig. Because of the slower speed and better boat control, you can keep your bait in the fish zone more easily than you could by forward trolling.

Keep your bail open and hold the line with your finger when slip-sinker fishing. A smallmouth often makes a fast run after it grabs the bait. If your bail is closed, you cannot release your line in time.

When the fish stops running, reel up the slack until you feel some resistance before setting the hook. Smallmouth may swim a long distance and put a lot of slack in the line. If you do not reel up the slack, you will not have enough leverage to set the hook.

SMALLMOUTH often rocket toward the surface after grabbing the bait. With a slip-sinker rig (inset), the sinker stays near the bottom, resulting in a lot of slack. If the fish takes more than 10 feet of line and continues to run, quickly reel up the slack and set the hook.

How to Hook Bait for Split-shot and Slip-sinker Fishing

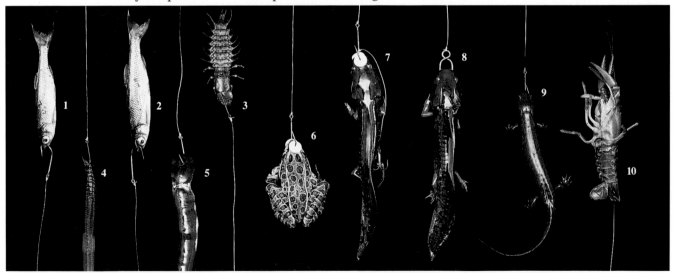

HOOK a minnow (1) through the lips or (2) eyes with a size 2 to 6 hook; a hellgrammite (3) under the collar with a size 4 or 6 hook; a nightcrawler (4) through the head with a size 6 or 8 hook; a leech (5) near the sucker with a size 6 or 8 hook; a frog (6) through the lips with a size 2 or 4 hook and bait-saver tabs (page 123); a waterdog (7) through the lips with a size 2 or 4 hook, tabs and a size 12 stinger, or (8) with a size 2 Super Hook pinched over the head; a spring lizard (9) through the lips and out the eye with a size 2 or 4 hook; and a crayfish (10) through the tail and out the belly with a size 2 or 4 long-shank hook.

Slip-bobber Fishing

A slip-bobber rig is a good choice when smallmouth are not in the mood to feed. Even a full-bellied smallmouth will take a nip at a stationary bait if it wiggles in front of his nose long enough.

You can adjust your slip-bobber knot to keep your bait dangling just off bottom, so the rig works well over rocks or other snags. And, when smallmouth are tightly schooled, a slip-bobber rig enables you to keep your bait in the fish zone more of the time than you could with any other method.

When your bobber goes down, wait a few seconds, tighten your line until you feel weight, then set the hook. If you wait too long, the smallmouth will feel resistance and let go.

ADJUST your slip-bobber rig (inset) so the bait dangles 6 to 12 inches off bottom. Slide the bobber stop (arrow) up the line the same distance you want the bait to hang below the surface. About 18 inches above the hook, pinch on enough split-shot so the bobber barely floats.

HOOK a leech (1) through the middle with a size 6 hook; a minnow (2) below the dorsal with a size 4 hook; a crayfish (3) through the tail with a size 2 or 4 hook; a hellgrammite (4) under the collar with a size 4 or 6 hook; and a crawler (5) through the middle with a size 6 hook.

Tips for Fishing with Live Bait

KEEP shiners alive in warm weather by adding ice to your minnow bucket to chill the water. Try to keep the water at about the same temperature it was at the bait shop.

CARRY your leeches in a specially designed bucket that enables you to change water easily. When you lift the inner bucket, water drains through the holes, but the leeches stay in.

HOLD your bait on the hook and keep it from covering the hook gap by threading on tabs made from a (1) rubber band or (2) plastic lid. Or, tie rubber bands on the shank (3).

Freelining

Freelining allows you to present your bait more naturally than you could with any other technique. Simply tie on a hook and let the bait swim about with no sinker to restrict its movement.

Lob-cast your bait so it alights over a shallow rock bar, or alongside a boulder, log or some other type of shallow-water cover. Let the bait swim freely, but keep your line just tight enough so you will feel a bite. After a minute or two, twitch the bait or move it a short distance, then let it swim again.

Use a fine-wire hook and 4- to 6-pound mono for freelining. A thick-shanked hook will weight down the bait and heavier line will prevent it from swimming naturally.

HOOK a minnow (1) in the tail with a size 4 hook; a leech (2) in the sucker end with a size 6 hook; a crayfish (3) through the tail with a size 2 hook; a frog (4) through the hind leg with a size 2 hook; and a grasshopper or cricket (5) under the collar with a size 6 hook.

KEEP some tension on your line when freelining with a crayfish. If you allow the crayfish to move about as it pleases, it will crawl under a rock or log and hide. Some fishermen remove the pincers to keep the crayfish from holding onto objects on the bottom.

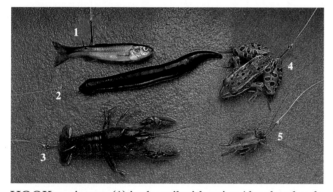

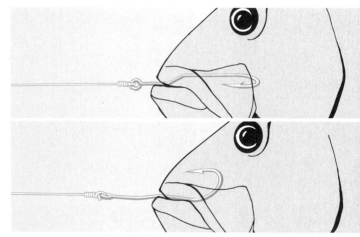

ADD some type of attractor when smallmouth refuse a plain bait. Popular attractors include: (1) a spinner, clevis and beads; (2) a small *corkie*, which slides freely on the line; (3) a piece of yarn snelled onto the hook; and (4) a small live-rubber skirt.

TRY a *cam-action* hook if you are missing too many fish. When a smallmouth clamps down on the bait, the hook lies flat on its side (top). But when you set the hook, the cam design causes the point to rotate up or down so it will penetrate the fish's jaw (bottom).

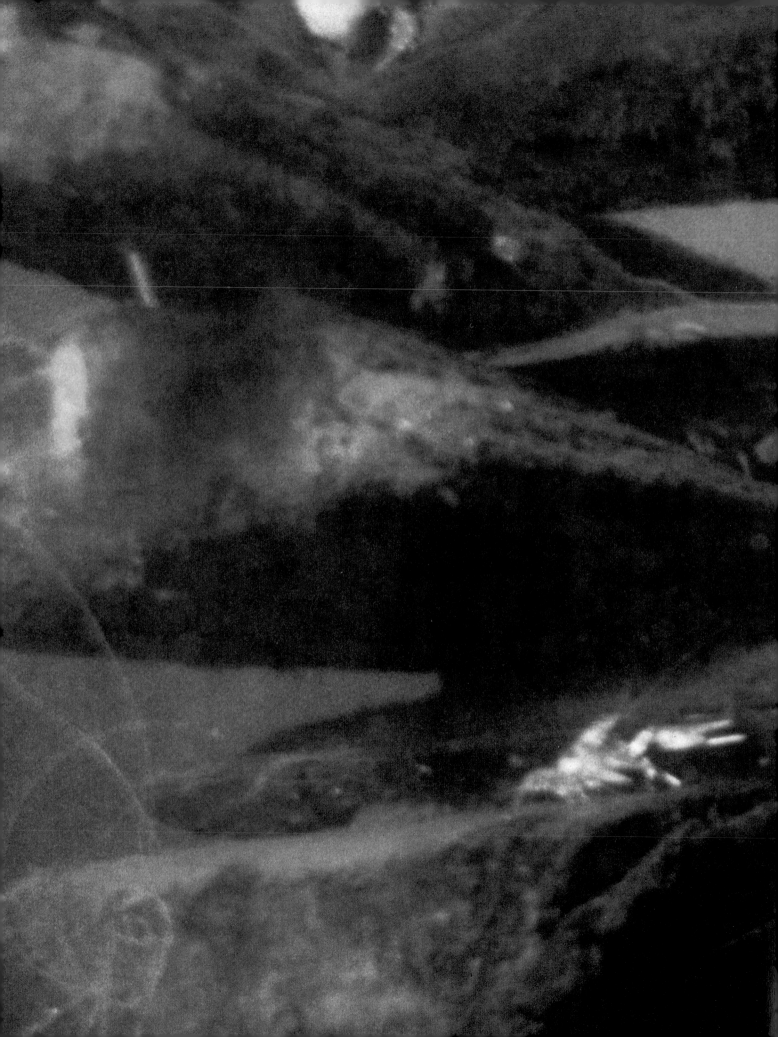

Techniques for Special Situations

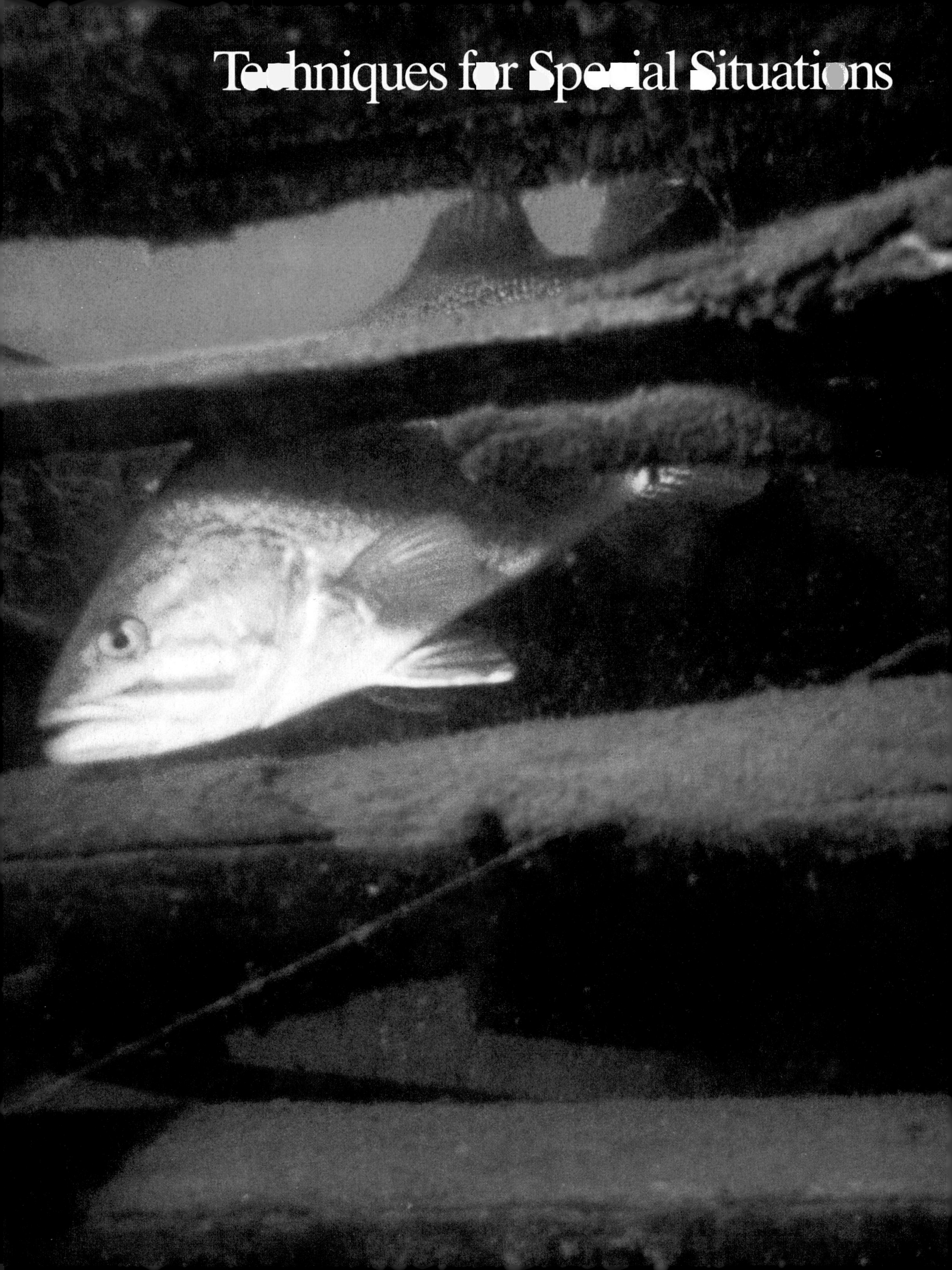

Fishing During the Spawning Period

Smallmouth fishing is never easier than during the spawning period. When males are defending their nests, they will attack anything that comes too close, including an angler's lure or bait. On occasion, a wading fisherman has been startled when a smallmouth swam up and bumped his boots.

Catching the females is not so easy. They stay in the vicinity of the nest before spawning, but in deeper water. If the nests are in 2 feet of water, for instance, the females may be in 8 feet, usually on the first significant drop-off out from the nesting area. Females do not feed much during this period, so they pay little attention to a fisherman's offerings. But if you work this deeper water thoroughly, you may coax a few to bite.

Females are even more difficult to catch once they have finished spawning. You may catch a few starting about two weeks later, but in some waters, they refuse to bite for three weeks or longer.

Nest-guarding males will take almost any kind of lure or bait, especially if it appears to pose a threat. As a result, precise casting is a must. A male will attack a lure or bait that passes directly over its nest or a few inches to the side, but it will ignore one a

Approximate Date of Spawning Peak at Different Latitudes

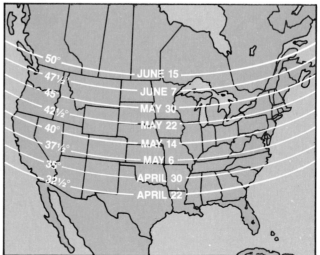

SPAWNING takes place much earlier in the South than in the North. At a given latitude, smallmouth may spawn several weeks earlier in a warm spring than in a cold one and a month earlier in a shallow lake than in a deep one.

LOOK for circular spots on bottom (foreground) that reveal the location of smallmouth nests. They may be dark or light, depending on bottom type. Once you find a nest, chances are others will be at about the same depth.

few feet to the side. Although subtle colors work best for smallmouth most of the year, bright or fluorescent colors often work better around spawning time.

Small jigs, from 1/16 to 1/8 ounce, are effective at depths down to 10 feet. The breathing action of a marabou jig gives it an especially threatening look. A jig also has a more menacing look if it sinks slowly. You can reduce the sink rate by adding a large, soft-plastic tail or by using a tin-head jig instead of a lead head.

Single-blade spinnerbaits, usually 1/4-ounce models, are a good choice where the nest is surrounded by weeds, logs or brush. Reel until the lure is over the nest, then stop and let it helicopter. The male will probably grab it before it reaches bottom. Standard spinners work well over a clean bottom, and their smaller size may be more appealing.

Surface lures like propbaits, poppers and divers also work well. Let them rest motionless over the nest for 30 seconds or more before retrieving. Often you can coax a strike by jiggling the lure so it ripples the surface without moving ahead. Floating minnow plugs can be fished much the same way, or they can be retrieved faster to reach smallmouth at depths down to 5 feet.

Fly fishing can be extremely effective because you can cast with pinpoint accuracy. And you can cover a large area quickly because you do not have to reel in after each cast. In shallow water, a nest-guarding male will usually hit a popper, diver or other bug

fished on a floating line. In deeper water, a jigging fly on a floating line or a streamer on a sink-tip line would work better.

Normally, live bait is not necessary to catch spawning males. But it may catch more females. Any type of live bait will work, but leeches, waterdogs, and spring lizards on split-shot rigs are most effective. Smallmouth consider any salamander-type bait a menace to their nests.

When planning a trip to catch spawning smallmouth, you should have an idea of when they spawn. If you arrive too early or too late, the males will not be on the nests. To get an idea of when smallmouth spawn in the waters you fish, check the spawning timetable on the opposite page. To find likely spawning areas in your waters, refer to the seasonal-location section on pages 49 to 69.

Because of the male smallmouth's almost suicidal behavior, many conservation agencies close their waters to fishing during the spawning period. But many others believe that no significant harm comes from catching spawning smallmouth, so they leave the season open.

In areas where the season remains open, savvy fishermen release any smallmouth they catch. If you handle them carefully, males will return to their nests immediately when released. To eliminate the possibility of injuring the fish, file or bend back the barbs on your hooks. Some anglers have caught the same smallmouth two or three times, and it returned to the nest each time.

Tips for Catching Smallmouth During the Spawning Period

SLOW the sink rate of your spinnerbait by removing the blade and substituting a larger one. A Colorado-style blade has the slowest sink rate.

RIG the last 4 inches of a twister-tail worm Texas-style with a 1/16-ounce sinker. The tail will wiggle as the worm sinks slowly toward the nest.

TIP your jig with a leech if you cannot see the nest. A squirming leech is more threatening than a plain jig, so males will leave the nest to grab it.

Smallmouth
in the Weeds

Smallmouth often conceal themselves along the fringe of a weedbed as they lie in wait for unsuspecting baitfish.

Although smallmouth are not as weed-oriented as largemouth, weeds can be a key in locating them. Weeds make prime smallmouth habitat in oligotrophic lakes, especially if most of the lake basin is rocky. They are also important in rocky mesotrophic lakes. The rocky habitat holds some smallmouth, but you can generally catch more and bigger ones if you can find a sandy-bottomed hump, point or bay with sparse weed growth. The weeds support a different type of food chain: fewer insects and crayfish but more baitfish.

Weeds are not as important in most other types of waters. In lakes where weeds grow virtually everywhere in the shallows, smallmouth will seek the typical clean-bottomed habitat, such as rock piles and gravel patches.

Smallmouth may be found in both emergent and submerged vegetation, usually the types that grow on firm bottoms. Seldom will you find them in cattails or other weeds associated with soft bottoms. Low-growing or scattered weeds normally hold more smallmouth than tall or dense varieties. It may be that tall or dense weeds interfere with a smallmouth's ability to catch its prey.

The best smallmouth weeds are within easy reach of deep water. A band of weeds growing along a dropoff is much more likely to hold smallmouth than a large, weedy flat with no deep water nearby.

When a smallmouth takes your bait and winds itself around a stem, you will need fairly stout tackle and heavier-than-normal line to pull it free. Medium power to medium-heavy power spinning or baitcasting gear with 8- to 14-pound abrasion-resistant mono is suitable for most types of weeds.

Fishing in Bulrushes

These tough, round-stemmed plants grow on sand or gravel bottoms, usually in water from 2 to 5 feet deep. They extend 3 to 6 feet above the surface, so their total height may exceed 10 feet.

Smallmouth are found in and around bulrush beds mainly during the spawning season. But if the bulrushes border deep water, smallmouth may feed in them through the summer and into early fall.

Bulrushes by themselves do not provide much cover, so the best stands have plenty of rocks or logs. They also have numerous open pockets, indentations along the margins, or boat lanes or other types of channels leading through them. Smallmouth hang around the edges of these openings so they can easily ambush baitfish. The openings also make it possible to present a lure without snagging.

When casting into a bulrush bed, try to keep the wind in your face. That way, the bulrushes will be bending toward you, so your lure will tend to slide off the stems instead of snagging.

In addition to the lures shown on this page, other choices for fishing in bulrushes include surface plugs like chuggers and propbaits, Texas-rigged plastic worms, fly-fishing lures like jigging flies and divers, and split-shot rigs with weedless hooks.

TWITCH a floating minnow plug over the surface rather than using a steady retrieve. By twitching it, you can snake it through the bulrushes without snagging. If you reel too fast, the hooks will catch on the tough stems. The same type of presentation works with a propbait.

WORK deep bulrush beds with a 1/16- to 1/8-ounce brush-guard jig tipped with pork rind or some type of live bait. When smallmouth are not active, a light jig fluttering to bottom is more effective than a minnow plug or propbait twitched on the surface.

RETRIEVE a small spinnerbait through the bulrushes by reeling steadily, pausing to let it helicopter when you reach an open pocket, a boulder or a log. A spinnerbait seldom snags in bulrushes, so you can work it through the thickest part of the bed.

Fishing in Cabbage

Given a choice, smallmouth prefer the broad-leaved varieties of cabbage to the narrow-leaved types. Normally, smallmouth are found in cabbage beds in 6 to 14 feet of water.

Smallmouth are most likely to use cabbage beds from late spring through early fall. Later, when the cabbage turns brown, they retreat to deeper water.

The cabbage beds best suited to smallmouth are those where the individual plants are spaced several feet apart. Smallmouth are rarely found in dense beds where the plants grow close enough together to form a canopy.

Cabbage has crisp leaves that shatter easily. A fast-moving lure will usually rip through the leaves without fouling, and a slow-moving lure can be freed with a sharp tug.

Surface techniques are usually not as effective as mid-water or bottom techniques for fishing in cabbage. Besides the lures and rigs shown on this page, you can also catch smallmouth in cabbage on spinnerbaits and crankbaits.

TEXAS-RIG a grubtail (inset) to make it completely weedless. Peg the sinker with a piece of toothpick so it will not slide up the line when the lure rides over the leaves. If the sinker slides up, you will lose feel.

RIP a light jig with an open hook through a cabbage bed. The jig may catch on the leaves, but you can free it with a sharp tug. An open hook snags more often than a brushguard hook, but increases your hooking percentage.

TIE a special slip-sinker rig (inset) for working live bait through cabbage. With a brushguard hook and a cone sinker, the rig will rarely snag. In sparse cabbage, you may be able to use an open hook.

Fishing in Sandgrass

Sandgrass or muskgrass, technically called *Chara,* is a brittle, narrow-leaved plant that grows in water as deep as 35 feet. It often forms a blanket several inches thick covering a large area.

You can find some smallmouth in sandgrass in summer, but the best time is late fall. Sandgrass grows in deeper water than practically any other aquatic plant, and often is the only deep-water cover.

Large sandgrass flats may hold some smallmouth, but these areas are difficult to fish because the small-mouth are scattered. A deep hump or point carpeted with sandgrass would be a better choice.

Fishing in sandgrass is tricky. If you use a jig or live-bait rig, the hook catches on the tiny branchlets. When you pull, one branchlet snaps and the hook stops abruptly as it catches on another. This creates a tugging sensation hard to distinguish from a bite.

Almost any deep-running lure or live-bait rig will work in sandgrass. But you must be alert for excess drag, because small pieces of sandgrass will often cling to your hook.

RETRIEVE a deep-running crankbait over sparse sandgrass. Make sure the lip occasionally digs bottom. The lure usually rips through cleanly, and the bottom disturbance may trigger a strike.

Fishing in Other Weeds

Although smallmouth prefer the previously shown weeds, they will use many other weeds when their favorite types are not available.

Savvy smallmouth anglers do not hesitate to try any weeds that offer food and cover. Even weeds not normally associated with smallmouth, such as lily pads, can be productive at times. Shown below are some of the other weeds in which smallmouth may be found.

MILFOIL. The feather-veined leaves grow in whorls around the stem. These plants resemble coontail, but coontail leaves are forked.

WILD CELERY. The long leaves have a light-colored center stripe. Small flowers grow at the tops of long, spiraling stems.

CANADA WATERWEED. The leaves are shorter and wider than those of milfoil or coontail, and an individual strand is much narrower.

131

Smallmouth in Woody Cover

Woody cover makes ideal smallmouth habitat because it harbors smallmouth foods like insects and minnows in addition to providing shade and protection from larger predators. In rivers, woody cover also creates pockets of slack water where smallmouth can get out of the current.

The best woody cover is in areas where smallmouth can fulfill all of their needs without moving too far. Consequently, a fallen tree on a rubble or boulder bottom would attract more smallmouth than a similar tree on a mucky bottom. Crayfish and aquatic insect larvae living on the rubble or boulder bottom make it more appealing.

If the fallen tree is adjacent to deep water, it would be even more appealing. Then, smallmouth could easily move to deeper water should the light become too bright or the water temperature too warm.

Smallmouth make use of many kinds of woody cover. Besides fallen trees, possible smallmouth hangouts include standing timber, submerged logs, standing or toppled stumps, flooded shoreline brush, beaver lodges and piles of beaver cuttings.

TREES, LOGS AND STUMPS. Experts know that certain trees, logs and stumps hold more smallmouth than others that look practically the same. Part of the difference lies in the bottom composition and the depth of the surrounding water, but there are also differences in the cover itself.

Smallmouth prefer cover that offers overhead protection as well as shade, so a toppled tree with a thick trunk and limbs is more attractive than one with a thinner trunk and limbs, assuming that the habitat is similar.

Standing timber offers some shade, but little overhead cover. It often draws largemouth, but is not as attractive to smallmouth. The lack of overhead cover also explains why a log lying flat on the bottom attracts fewer smallmouth than one that is somehow propped up from the bottom.

FLOODED BRUSH. In spring, when river or reservoir levels rise high enough to cover shoreline vegetation, smallmouth move into flooded brush. They stay in the brush as long as the water continues to rise or remains stable. But as soon as it begins to fall, they move deeper.

Fishermen sink brush piles into deep water, but the water where you find naturally flooded brush is usually shallow. Brush will survive seasonal flooding, but once it is flooded permanently it soon rots away. This explains why new reservoirs have an abundance of brushy cover, but old reservoirs have very little, if any.

Seasonally flooded brush is usually too dense for smallmouth to hide between the branches. Instead of attempting to work your bait or lure through the brush, concentrate on any pockets or fish the edges.

BEAVER LODGES. The idea of fishing around beaver lodges never occurs to most smallmouth fishermen. The areas where beavers build their lodges usually look too shallow and marshy for smallmouth. What many anglers do not realize is that beavers excavate deep entrance holes and runs leading into their lodges. The combination of deep water and overhead logs and brush makes excellent smallmouth habitat.

Another reason that smallmouth like beaver lodges: the mud used to cement the logs and brush attracts many types of burrowing aquatic insects, so smallmouth enjoy a built-in food supply.

Smallmouth also hang around beaver feed beds, especially in small streams. These piles of fresh cuttings are usually close to the lodge.

When fishing in woody cover, remember the old adage "no guts, no glory." To catch the biggest smallmouth, you must work the thickest, shadiest part of the cover. This usually means casting into small openings in the branches instead of casting around the edges. There is no way to avoid getting snagged and losing some lures; that's the price you must pay for success.

If you do get snagged, simply break your line and tie on another lure. If you jerk the branches back and forth or move your boat into the cover to retrieve your lure, you will surely spook the smallmouth.

The techniques for fishing in woody cover are similar to those used in weeds. Most fishermen cast with snag-resistant artificials like spinnerbaits, brushguard jigs and Texas-rigged soft plastics. When rigging Texas style, peg your cone sinker to keep it from sliding away from your worm or grub. Pegging gives you better feel and reduces snagging.

You can fish live bait in woody cover by freelining (page 123), or by casting a split-shot or cone-sinker rig. Use a brushguard hook or a fine-wire hook that will bend enough to pull free if you get snagged.

If there are pockets in the cover, you can flycast with bass bugs or jigging flies, jig vertically with a jigging spoon, twitch a surface plug or minnow plug through the openings, or dangle live bait from a bobber. Other techniques for fishing in woody cover are shown on the opposite page.

Fishing in woody cover demands heavy tackle, like a medium-heavy or heavy power baitcasting outfit with 12- to 20-pound abrasion-resistant mono. With heavy tackle, you are better able to free a snagged lure. And you can horse a smallmouth out of the cover before it has a chance to wrap your line around a branch.

How to Find Submerged Woody Cover

LOOK for a tree line along the shore of a reservoir, then visually extend the line into the water. Smallmouth often hold along the edge of the submerged trees.

CHECK the location of timber and brush in your favorite smallmouth water at normal water stage (top) or during a drawdown. Then, you will have a better idea of what is beneath the surface when the water is higher (bottom).

WATCH for collapsed banks in reservoirs, pits or big rivers. If the remaining bank is covered with timber or brush, there is a good chance of finding submerged timber and brush where the bank slid into the water.

Techniques for Casting to Overhanging Limbs (right-handed angler)

UNDERHAND CAST. Use an underhand cast for placing your lure into an opening beneath overhanging limbs that would be difficult to reach from either side.

BACKHAND CAST. Use a backhand cast for placing your lure beneath branches that have an opening under the left-hand side.

FOREHAND CAST. Use a forehand cast for placing your lure beneath branches that have an opening under the right-hand side.

FLIPPIN'. Use the flippin' technique to place your lure into tight spots. Flippin' is very accurate because you hold the line in your left hand to control distance.

Tips for Fishing in Woody Cover

DABBLE live bait into woody cover using a ½- to 1-ounce sinker. If you get snagged, let the sinker drop so its weight jerks the hook free.

HOLD your boat in position with a brush clamp. With the clamp, you will not spook fish with your anchor and you can easily move to another spot.

USE a jigging fly or diver with a mono brushguard. The mono is flexible enough that it does not reduce your hooking percentage.

Smallmouth around Manmade Features

When reservoirs are filled, the rising water covers numerous manmade objects that later become good cover for many types of fish, including smallmouth bass. Manmade objects also attract smallmouth in natural lakes and rivers.

Stone or concrete foundations, particularly those located on hills, are considered the top smallmouth-fishing spots in many reservoirs. Smallmouth feed in and around the foundation, then retreat to the deeper water surrounding the hill.

Submerged railroad grades are made to order for smallmouth. The coarse gravel on top of the grade makes a good feeding area, and the sharp-sloping sides offer shade. Railroad bridges over roads and waterways are usually removed before a reservoir is filled, and the gaps in the grade make good hiding spots for smallmouth.

Exhumed cemeteries should also be checked out. Smallmouth are drawn to the remaining dirt piles. Often, cemeteries are surrounded by standing timber, so smallmouth can hide among the trees and dart into the clearing to ambush prey.

Submerged roads made of concrete or asphalt are prime smallmouth spots, especially if the roadway material is broken up. The rubble that remains will draw crayfish, minnows and insects. And the adjoining ditches give smallmouth a deeper resting area. Roadbeds located in shallow water make good spawning habitat.

Fish attractors, especially those constructed with brush, draw large numbers of insects and baitfish. So it is no surprise that they also attract smallmouth. Attractors placed along a drop-off or the edge of a creek channel usually hold more smallmouth than those placed on a flat bottom.

In the Great Lakes and other large natural lakes, smallmouth can be found around shipwrecks, collapsed seawalls and jetties, docks, lighthouses and ship channels, especially those blasted from rock.

Manmade features found in rivers are covered in the river-fishing section (pages 141 to 145).

You can fish manmade features using practically any technique that works for similar natural cover. To fish a brushy fish attractor, for instance, refer to the section on woody cover (pages 132 to 135). To fish a broken-up roadbed, see the section on fishing on a rocky bottom (pages 138-139).

MANMADE FEATURES that offer overhead protection are prime smallmouth hangouts. Good examples include wooden fish cribs; culverts and other discharge structures; and docks, especially covered ones.

How to Find Manmade Features

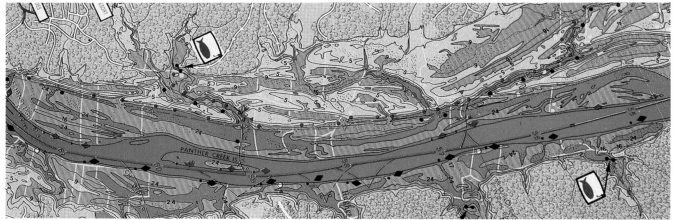

STUDY a lake map to find manmade features. This map shows submerged buildings (yellow squares), roads (yellow lines), cemeteries (yellow Xs), fish attractors (red symbols), and old ponds (dark blue ovals). The old river channel is indicated with a dashed red line. Darker shades of blue indicate deeper water.

LOCATE fish attractors by looking for signs or specially marked buoys. In many reservoirs, a cluster or line of brush shelters (left) is marked with a sign on shore (middle). These shelters are shown during a drawdown period and will be submerged once the water rises. Sometimes, shelters near shore are identified by marks on trees. Fish attractors located farther away from shore are often marked with a buoy bearing a fish symbol (right).

Tips for Fishing Around Manmade Features

WORK an abutment by counting a jig down to various depths. Smallmouth usually stay on the shady side, but not necessarily near bottom.

CAST parallel to a submerged fenceline to catch smallmouth. Fencelines that slope rapidly into deep water are the best producers.

TOSS your bait or lure into the shade of a covered dock. Covered docks are especially productive on sunny days in spring and early summer.

Smallmouth in Rocks & Boulders

Smallmouth spend more of their time around rocks and boulders than any other freshwater gamefish. Fishing in this snaggy cover can be extremely frustrating, but there are many techniques to help you keep the problem of snagging to a minimum.

The best way to avoid snags is to keep your bait or lure riding just above bottom. Smallmouth hiding among the rocks are accustomed to darting upward to grab food, so there is no need to drag bottom.

If you attempt to drag your bait or lure along a bottom strewn with rocks, you will always get some snags, even if you use sinkers and hooks that manufacturers claim to be snagless.

Keeping your bait or lure just above the bottom sounds easy, but requires a great deal of concentration. Many fishermen are not comfortable unless they can feel the bottom, so they continually drop their rod tip back to test the depth. Before long, the sinker or lure will wedge into the rocks.

To avoid snags, you must resist the urge to continually feel the bottom. Instead, touch bottom once, then reel up a foot or two and try to maintain that depth. When casting, try to find the retrieve speed that will keep the lure or bait just off bottom. If you are trolling or drifting, watch your depth finder closely. When the depth changes, adjust your line accordingly. Should you lose your concentration and fail to reel in line when the water gets shallower, you will probably get snagged. Should you fail to let out more line when it gets deeper, your bait or lure will pass too high above the fish.

When casting, use the lightest sinker that will take your bait to the bottom. This way, you can retrieve slowly, yet keep the sinker gliding above the rocks. If you are using artificials, select one intended for the depth at which you are fishing. If you are casting into 5 feet of water, for instance, you will get fewer snags with a 1/16-ounce jig than with a 1/4-ounce jig.

When trolling in deep water, use a relatively heavy sinker so you can keep your line nearly vertical. This allows you to hold the sinker just off bottom, and the steep line angle reduces the chances of the sinker wedging in the rocks. The same principle applies to artificials. And keeping your line as short as possible makes it easier to feel your lure tick bottom.

Although nothing is completely snag-free, you can substantially reduce the number of snags by using the right tackle. If you rig your bait on a floating jig head and use a bottom-walking sinker, for instance, you will get only about half as many snags as you would with a standard hook and sinker. And a long-lipped crankbait will deflect off the rocks better than a short-lipped model.

If snagging continues to be a problem, you can always use some type of snag remover or plug knocker. One of the simplest gadgets for freeing a snag is a large clip-on sinker attached to a string (shown on opposite page).

When you combine the right tackle with the right technique, snagging will become the exception rather than the rule. And your smallmouth fishing will become more enjoyable and more successful.

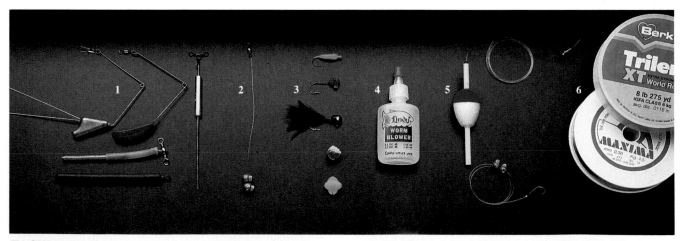

TACKLE for fishing in rocky cover includes: (1) snag-resistant sinkers; (2) a dropper rigged with split-shot that slide off the line if they get snagged; (3) floating jig heads and other floats that lift your bait off the bottom; (4) a worm blower, for inflating a crawler to make it ride higher; (5) a slip-bobber rig, which can be adjusted to keep your bait dangling just above the rocks; and (6) abrasion-resistant mono.

Tips for Fishing in Rocks and Boulders

MAKE your own snag-resistant sinker using a piece of coat hanger. Pound one end flat, drill a small hole and insert a snap-swivel.

USE a long rod, 8 to 8½ feet. Then, if you get snagged, you can reach out and change the angle of pull without moving your boat.

UNSNAG your lure by clipping a removable sinker attached to a string onto your line. Lower the sinker fast; the impact will free your lure.

River Fishing

Some anglers maintain that river smallmouth fight more than their counterparts in lakes; others say that it just seems that way because of the flowing water. Either way, you are in for some excitement when you hook a river smallmouth.

In many parts of the country, river smallmouth offer an almost untapped fishing opportunity. If an area has a lot of natural lakes or reservoirs, these waters draw the vast majority of fishing pressure.

Smallmouth inhabit a wide variety of flowing waters, ranging in size from small creeks only 10 feet wide to the largest rivers. The best smallmouth populations are in medium-sized rivers with recognizable pool and riffle areas. Big, slow-moving rivers with silty channels rarely have good populations of smallmouth bass.

The best time to fish rivers is during periods of low water. Smallmouth will be concentrated in deep holes and easy to find. When the water is high, they could be almost anywhere. Smallmouth bite better when the water is rising or stable than when it is falling. But if a torrential rain causes the water to rise quickly and become muddy, fishing is poor.

Smallmouth in rivers tend to be in shallower water than those in lakes. Most smallmouth rivers have enough current so there is continuous mixing, so smallmouth cannot find cooler water by going deep. Except in late fall and winter, when they move into deep holes, river smallmouth are seldom found at depths exceeding 10 feet.

River smallmouth avoid strong current, but they will tolerate a moderate current. In rivers that have both smallmouth and walleyes, smallmouth are found in water that moves slightly faster. In many cases they inhabit the same pool, but smallmouth spend more time in the upper portion of the pool, while walleyes are in deeper, slacker water farther downstream. Smallmouth and spotted bass divide up the habitat in much the same way.

With the exception of heavy rains, weather seems to have less effect on smallmouth in rivers than in lakes. They continue to bite despite cold fronts, severe thunderstorms or extremely hot weather.

The ideal rig for most river fishing is a 14- to 16-foot jon boat with a 10- to 15-horsepower outboard. A jon boat draws only a few inches of water, so it will float over shallow riffles. Yet the flat-bottomed design gives it good stability.

If the river has deep holes, a flasher comes in handy. But in most river-fishing situations, you can visually identify the prime smallmouth spots.

Many rivers can be fished without a boat and a lot of expensive equipment. All you need is a rod and reel, a few lures and a pair of hipboots or waders. In summer, you can get by with shorts and tennis shoes.

How to Recognize a Good Smallmouth River

HIGH-GRADIENT rivers are not suited to smallmouth because the current is too fast. Smallmouth are seldom found in a river whose *gradient,* or slope, exceeds 25 feet per mile.

LOW-GRADIENT rivers, with a slope less than 2 feet per mile, hold few smallmouth. The slow current allows the water to get too warm, and results in a silty, flat bottom.

MODERATE-GRADIENT rivers, with a slope of 7 to 20 feet per mile, support the most smallmouth. They normally have cool temperatures and plenty of riffles and pools.

SIDE-CAST a weighted nymph under overhanging branches in a pool. Smallmouth lie beneath the branches waiting for insects to drop into the water, and will usually strike when the fly hits the surface or soon after it sinks.

Fishing Techniques for River Smallmouth

The secret to catching river smallmouth is learning to read the water. Eddies caused by boulders, log-jams, pilings and other above-water objects that break the current are easy to recognize. And with a little experience, you can also recognize eddies caused by underwater obstructions.

Every river has a few key spots that always hold smallmouth. Once you discover such a spot, you can catch the fish that are there, and more will move in to take their place. Some always hold big small-mouth, others only little ones.

After fishing a stretch of river once or twice, a river-fishing expert can identify practically all of these prime spots. By concentrating his efforts on these spots and bypassing less productive ones, he can catch as many smallmouth in an hour as the average angler could in a day.

Once you learn to identify these prime locations, the rest is easy. Smallmouth in rivers are generally not as fussy as those in lakes. They are conditioned to grab food as it drifts by, so they do not take much time to make up their mind.

Tips for Catching River Smallmouth

DRAG a heavy chain to slow your drift speed. Attach about 4 feet of logging chain to a rope, then lower it to bottom (left). You can regulate the angle at which the boat drifts by attaching the chain rope at different positions along another rope running from the bow to the stern (right). To drift with the bow pointing upstream, attach the chain rope toward the bow; to drift with the bow downstream, attach it toward the stern. Most experts believe that the chain does not spook the smallmouth. In fact, some think that the sound attracts them.

The lead-head jig is probably the most consistent producer of river smallmouth. One of the major advantages of a jig is that it sinks quickly, so it will reach bottom before the current sweeps it away from the spot you are trying to fish.

A ⅛-ounce jig works well in pools or eddies as deep as 7 feet. In deeper or swifter water, you may need a ¼- to ⅜-ounce jig. You can reach bottom more easily if you angle your casts upstream and retrieve downstream. But if the current is slow enough, it pays to cast downstream and retrieve upstream. Your jig will have better action and you will get fewer snags. However you retrieve the jig, always keep it bouncing bottom.

Standard spinners also work well for river smallmouth. Because they are conditioned to respond so quickly at the sight of food, the flash of a spinner blade immediately draws their attention. But standard spinners are limited mainly to shallow water. Unless the water is very shallow, angle your casts upstream. If you attempt to cast downstream, the water resistance causes the blade to turn too fast and forces the lure to the surface.

Small spinnerbaits are better than standard spinners for casting into snaggy cover like logjams, fallen trees or brush piles.

Crankbaits and minnow plugs allow you to cover a lot of water quickly. You can cast to pools, eddies and riffles while drifting or wading. Or you can troll a long stretch of uniform cover, like a riprap bank.

Select a crankbait or minnow plug suited to the type of water you are fishing. A short-lipped floating minnow plug is an excellent choice for cranking through the riffle at the upper end of a pool, but a deep-diving crankbait is more effective for fishing the pool itself.

The best way to work a pool is to cast into the fast water at the upper end, then crank the plug downstream so it moves faster than the current. Smallmouth are accustomed to lying at the upper end and grabbing food as it drifts into the pool.

Fly fishing is an excellent technique for river smallmouth because you can cast to precise spots, like a small pocket below a boulder. Subsurface flies such as streamers, crayfish and leech flies, and nymphs are the top choices. In summer, when smallmouth feed heavily on floating insects, bass bugs and dry flies also work well.

River fishermen also use a variety of live-bait rigs. A slip-sinker rig works best for large baits, like frogs and crayfish, because you can let the fish run and give it ample time to swallow the bait. A split-shot rig is better suited to smaller baits, like leeches and nightcrawlers. Use just enough weight to keep the bait drifting naturally along the bottom. When you feel a bite, simply drop your rod tip back, then set the hook. A slip-bobber rig is a good choice for fishing an eddy. Set the bobber to the right depth, then let the current sweep it around. A slip-bobber rig is ideal for hellgrammites and crayfish, because it keeps them from crawling under the rocks.

REDUCE your chance of snagging by hooking your bait on a floating jig head and adding just enough split-shot to make the bait sink. The hook will ride above the rocks and the shot will barely tick the bottom as the rig drifts downstream with the current.

LOOK for smallmouth around heated discharges from power plants or municipal treatment plants during the winter months. The discharge water may be 70°F or higher, so smallmouth will be active enough to strike fast-moving lures such as crankbaits and minnow plugs.

143

LAUNCH your boat at the upper end of the stretch you want to fish. Before launching, check the water stage. High water is dangerous; low water makes it difficult to float.

WORK the edges of the fast water below the dam with a ⅛- to ¼-ounce round-head jig (inset). Cast upstream and bounce the jig along bottom as it drifts with the current.

SLIP downstream while maneuvering the boat toward cover on either side of the stream. Then, cast a shallow-running crankbait (inset) into pockets above and below the boulders.

How to Make a Float Trip

One of the most enjoyable and most effective methods of fishing a river is to make a float trip. By floating, you can get away from the crowd and fish parts of the river that receive little fishing pressure.

If the river is deep enough, a float trip can be a one-man operation. You float as far downstream as you wish, then simply motor back up. But if there are a lot of riffles, you may not be able to motor upstream without hitting bottom. In this case, the trip requires a partner with a second vehicle.

The usual strategy is to drive both vehicles to a take-out location a distance downstream of the spot where you will put in. Leave one vehicle, then tow the boat to your put-in spot. When you have floated down to the take-out spot, pull the boat up on shore, then drive back to pick up the other vehicle.

Another option is to leave a bicycle at the downstream end, then pedal it back to your car after you complete the float.

On the average, you can cover about 7 miles on a day's float. If you attempt to cover much more, you will probably have to bypass some good spots. After floating a stretch of river once, you will have a much better idea of how far you can go the next time.

Although a jon boat is the best choice for a float trip, many fishermen use canoes or small semi-Vs. On a two-vehicle float, you can get by with a pair of oars instead of an outboard. But a small outboard comes in handy for motoring upstream to make a second float through a productive area.

If you catch several smallmouth in a certain pool or eddy, you should anchor and work the spot more thoroughly. Or, pull your boat up on shore and fish the spot by wading.

CAST a ⅛- to ¼-ounce spinnerbait (inset) into pockets between the branches of a fallen tree or logjam. Let the lure sink enough that it bounces off the submerged limbs.

CATCH frogs along a marshy bank, then drift them on a slip-sinker rig (inset). Smallmouth lie in wait along the bank to grab frogs when they hop into the water.

ANCHOR upstream of a deep pool, then cast a bullet-head jig (inset) downstream. The jig cuts easily through current, so you can work it in the fast water at the head of the pool.

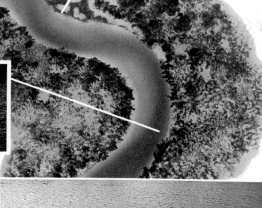

DRIFT along a deep stretch using a 3-way swivel rig (inset). Keep your line as nearly vertical as possible. If the sinker snags, you can break it off without losing the entire rig.

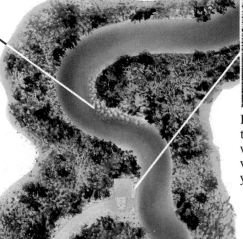

RETRIEVE a standard spinner with a size 1 or 2 blade (inset) over a shallow, rocky shoal. Angle your casts upstream; if you cast downstream, the blade may turn too fast.

PULL your boat up on shore and throw out the anchor. Drive upriver with your partner to get the other vehicle, then return with the trailer so you can load the boat.

Low-Clarity Water

Although smallmouth are generally found in clear water, there are times when you have to fish for them in water where you cannot see your lure more than a few inches below the surface. In eutrophic lakes (page 58) and big rivers (pages 68-69), low clarity is often a permanent situation. In smaller rivers and streams, heavy rains often cloud the water for days or weeks at a time.

When fishing for smallmouth in low-clarity water, keep the following principles in mind:

· Smallmouth are rarely found in water deeper than 10 feet, and are often at depths of 5 feet or less.

· Fishing is usually poor before dawn, after sunset and at night.

· Weather has less effect on smallmouth than it does in clear water, but calm, sunny weather is generally better than cloudy, windy weather.

· Artificial lures usually catch more smallmouth than live bait. Larger-than-normal lures work best.

· Lures that produce sound or vibration are more consistent smallmouth producers than those that do not. Bright or fluorescent colors usually work better than dull colors.

· Smallmouth are not as skittish as they are in clear water; line diameter is not much of a factor.

When planning your fishing strategy, it is important to know whether the low clarity is a permanent or temporary situation. If it is permanent, smallmouth will hold tight to cover, much as they do in clear water. And their senses are tuned to the low clarity, so they can detect minute vibrations that signal the presence of food. As a result, they will strike jigs and other lures that do not produce much sound.

If the low clarity is temporary, smallmouth roam the shallows looking for food. They may not notice a jig, but will be attracted by a sound-producing lure, like a rattling crankbait.

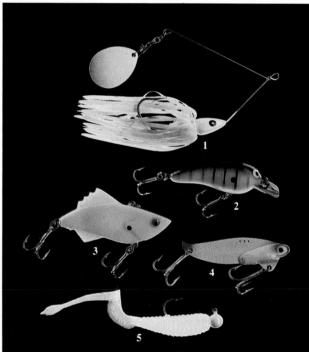

LURES for low-clarity water include: (1) ½-ounce spinnerbait; (2) shallow-running crankbait with rattles; (3) vibrating plug with rattles; (4) vibrating blade; (5) ⅛-ounce fluorescent jig head with 4-inch grub, for a slow sink rate in shallow water.

Ultra-Clear Water

If you fish for smallmouth early in the year, before algae blooms cloud the water, you may be able to see bottom in depths of 15 feet or more. In deep, cold lakes, the water may stay that clear all year. Streams often become very clear in fall, when runoff is minimal and cooler water reduces algal growth.

Smallmouth behave much differently in ultra-clear water than in moderate- to low-clarity water, so you must adjust your fishing strategy according to the following principles:

· Smallmouth are usually found much deeper than in low-clarity waters. In clear lakes, they normally inhabit depths of 15 to 30 feet. They feed in the shallows in dim-light periods, but stay in shallow water in midday only if they can find shady cover.

· Fishing is usually best in early morning, around dusk and at night. In clear southern reservoirs, experts do the majority of their fishing at night, especially during the summer.

· Weather has a major influence on smallmouth behavior. Overcast or windy days are usually best. Smallmouth bite better in periods of stable weather than in periods with frequent storms.

· Smallmouth seldom stray far from cover, so pinpoint casting and precise boat control are a must.

· Artificial lures that resemble real food are best. Dark or natural-colored lures usually outfish bright or fluorescent ones. Sound and vibration are less important than in low-clarity water.

· Smaller-than-normal lures generally work best.

· When fishing is slow, you may have no choice but to switch to live bait.

· Smallmouth are extremely skittish. It pays to hold noise and movement to a minimum and keep your distance from your casting target.

· Use 4- to 6-pound clear monofilament. Avoid using heavy leaders or large swivels.

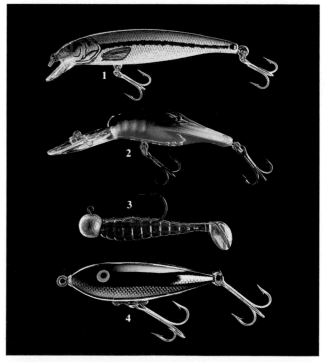

LURES for ultra-clear water include: (1) natural-finish minnow plug; (2) deep-diving, crayfish-pattern crankbait; (3) ⅜-ounce unpainted jig head with 2-inch, smoke-color tail, for a fast sink rate in deep water; (4) stickbait, for drawing smallmouth in deep water to the surface.

Night Fishing for Smallmouth

Night fishing is the best solution to a number of smallmouth-fishing problems. In ultra-clear waters, night fishing is productive because smallmouth do much of their feeding after dark, especially in summer. On heavily used lakes, the boat traffic often spooks smallmouth into deep water during the day, so they are forced to feed at night. Many southern smallmouth anglers prefer to fish at night because fishing is better and they can avoid sweltering daytime temperatures.

Night fishing is effective because smallmouth become much more aggressive under cover of darkness. Instead of holding tight to cover, they roam shallow shoals in search of food. And they are much less selective about what they strike, so you can use larger lures. In fact, bigger lures usually draw more strikes because they create more commotion.

When fishing at night, look for shallow shoals adjacent to the deeper areas where you catch smallmouth during the day. If you normally catch smallmouth in 12 feet of water off the tip of a point, for instance, try fishing on top of the point in about 5 feet of water after dark. Use the same pattern when fishing on offshore humps, shoreline breaks, or any other likely smallmouth hangouts.

If you can find a lot of points, humps and other likely structure in a small area, you can cover them quickly and reduce the distance you have to travel. This can be a big advantage, especially when night fishing in unfamiliar waters.

The depth where you find smallmouth will vary from night to night depending on the weather, but seldom will they be deeper than 10 feet. Often, they feed in only 2 or 3 feet of water.

Noisy lures are a good choice for night fishing. Lures like crawlers, propbaits and buzzbaits attract smallmouth by causing a lot of surface disturbance.

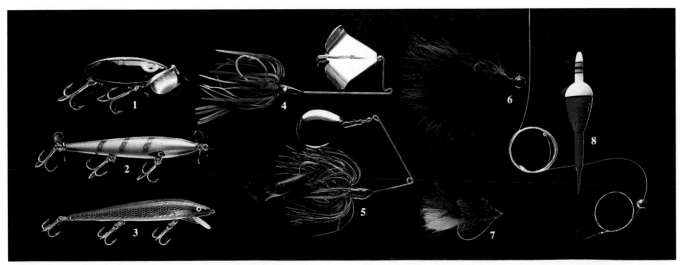

LURES AND RIGS for night fishing include: (1) crawler, (2) twin-bladed propbait, (3) short-lipped floating minnow plug, (4) buzzbait, (5) spinnerbait with size 5 blade and pork-frog trailer, (6) marabou jig, and (7) diver. All of these lures should be larger than those normally used for daytime fishing. For live-bait fishing, use a (8) lighted slip-bobber rig powered by a small lithium battery.

LIGHTED SWIMMING BEACHES and other well-lit areas along the shoreline can be excellent night-fishing spots. The lights attract swarms of insects which in turn draw shiners and other baitfish. Smallmouth move in to feed on the baitfish. Try casting with a noisy surface lure or large spinnerbait. Or, fly-cast with a diver.

Tips for Night Fishing

ILLUMINATE your line with an ultraviolet or *black light*. Be sure to use fluorescent mono to insure that the line shows up.

ATTACH your lure with a small U-shaped clip when fishing at night. The clip enables you to change lures quickly without tying a knot.

COVER your boat light with red cellophane. You can see well enough to change lures and unhook fish, yet your night vision is not affected.

BIG BAITS and lures work well for trophy smallmouth during the spawning period, in late fall and at night. In spring, when smallmouth are guarding their nests, larger baits and lures pose more of a threat. By late fall, the size of the smallmouth's natural food has increased, so they are accustomed to eating larger food items than they would earlier in the year. At night, big baits and lures are more likely to draw a smallmouth's attention than small ones. Larger-than-normal baits and lures are not recommended at other times.

Trophy Smallmouth

Anyone who spends much time fishing for trophy smallmouth has heard stories about the big one that got away. All respectable-sized smallmouth have a knack for throwing your hook, pulling your knot loose or breaking your line, but trophy smallmouth magnify the problem many times. So when you land a big one, there is a great feeling of accomplishment.

In most parts of the country, any smallmouth over 4 pounds is considered a trophy. But in mid-South reservoirs, a smallmouth must be 6 or 7 pounds to attain trophy status.

Waters that consistently produce big smallmouth have several things in common. Most have a significant area deeper than 50 feet. The deep structure has flat shelves for feeding and resting. If the structure plunges rapidly into deep water, it is of little value to smallmouth.

Good trophy waters seldom have heavy fishing pressure. Heavily fished waters produce few trophies because anglers catch the smallmouth before they have a chance to reach trophy size.

Most waters that produce a lot of trophy smallmouth do not have large smallmouth populations. Where smallmouth are numerous, there is a lot of competition for food and living space, so they do not grow as large. If you are interested in trophy fishing,

be prepared to put in some long days with only a strike or two for your efforts.

Waters where baitfish are the main food source are more likely to produce big smallmouth than those where the major food is crayfish or insects. And waters dominated by small baitfish are more likely to grow trophy smallmouth than those where most of the baitfish are large.

In mid-South reservoirs, for instance, threadfin shad make up a large part of the smallmouth's diet. Because threadfins seldom exceed 6 inches in length, smallmouth in these waters often grow to trophy size. Farther north, however, most reservoirs are dominated by gizzard shad which grow to 18 inches in length. The total food crop in any body of water is limited, and with so much of it consisting of oversized shad, smallmouth have less food that is usable and rarely grow to trophy size.

Your chances of catching a trophy smallmouth are generally better in reservoirs or natural lakes than in rivers. Most small- to medium-sized rivers lack the abundant baitfish crops needed for fast growth. Some big rivers, however, produce a fair number of trophy-caliber smallmouth.

It pays to do some research in advance to maximize your chances of locating good trophy water and being there at the time when the big ones are biting. State and provincial conservation agencies can give you some helpful hints, as can local bait shops and tackle stores. Outdoor magazines and newspapers that serve the area you are interested in can also help. Another source of information is the results of past fishing contests held in the area.

Most trophy hunters agree that big smallmouth bite best in spring, from 2 weeks before spawning until

Types of Waters Likely to Produce Trophy Smallmouth

MID-SOUTH RESERVOIRS have an ample food supply and a long growing season. Overfishing is seldom a problem because of their vast acreages and complex basins.

REMOTE NORTHERN LAKES have an abundance of rocky habitat ideal for smallmouth. Your chances for a trophy are best in lakes that cannot be fished with motorboats.

FERTILE NATURAL LAKES have poor spawning habitat for smallmouth, but abundant food. The few smallmouth that exist grow rapidly, but are overlooked by anglers.

spawning ends; on warm summer nights; and in fall, when the water temperature drops to about 60°F. Fall fishing remains good until the water cools to about 45°. Another good time to catch big smallmouth in streams is in late summer, when water levels are low and the fish are confined to deep pools.

Exactly where you find smallmouth during these periods depends on the type of water you are fishing. Refer to the seasonal-location section (pages 49 to 69).

As smallmouth get older, their personality and behavior patterns undergo dramatic changes. They lose their aggressive nature and become much more selective about what they eat. They hang tighter to cover and do more of their feeding at night. And they spend more of their time in deep water.

To catch big smallmouth with any degree of consistency, you must be aware of these changes and tailor your fishing techniques accordingly.

Although trophy-sized smallmouth are very skittish, the following steps will reduce the chances of spooking them:

· When they are in water less than 15 feet deep, do not run your outboard over them. Instead, hold your boat within casting distance with an electric motor or drop anchor.

· Avoid dropping anything in the boat.

· Keep a low profile and do not allow your shadow to fall on the spot you are fishing.

· Do not use big hooks or swivels, a heavy leader, or any type of highly visible terminal tackle.

· Use light, clear monofilament. Many trophy fishermen prefer 4-pound mono and few use mono heavier than 8 pound, unless they are fishing in heavy cover.

Big smallmouth almost always stay deeper than smaller ones. If you are catching 1- to 2-pound smallmouth in 10 feet of water, you will probably have to fish 15 to 20 feet deep to catch a trophy. But big smallmouth may feed in shallow water on a cloudy, windy day or at night.

In a given body of water, only a small fraction of the smallmouth spots produce trophy smallmouth. Typically, these spots have ample cover, easy access to deep water and a good food supply nearby. A spot that lacks any of these components will hold only small to average-sized smallmouth.

When you catch a big smallmouth, note the location carefully because the spot may hold more. Even if it does not, there is a good chance it will at a later date. Once a trophy smallmouth is removed, another usually moves in to take its place.

Where to Find Trophy Smallmouth

  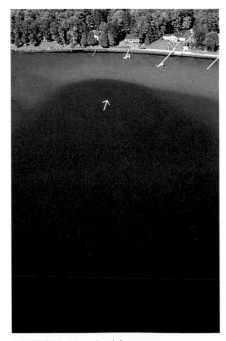

CAST directly into thick cover to catch the biggest smallmouth. The big fish force the smaller ones out of the best cover. If you fish only the edges, you will seldom catch a trophy.

LOOK for the steepest portion of a gradually sloping breakline. The biggest smallmouth prefer the sharpest break because they can reach deep water more easily.

CHECK any inside turns along a breakline. Plankton collects in the inside turns, drawing baitfish and other foods. The big smallmouth take over these preferred feeding zones.

If you know of some of these spots, work one for a few minutes, then move on to the next. If nothing happens, check them again in a few hours. Continue to check them throughout the day; the big smallmouth have to feed sometime. Concentrate only on these spots and resist the urge to try others that hold smaller fish which are easier to catch.

Although larger-than-normal baits and lures work well for trophy smallmouth at certain times (page 150), they are no more effective than smaller ones most of the year. And big baits and lures definitely reduce your chances of catching average-sized smallmouth. Bright or flashy lures catch big smallmouth at spawning time or in murky water, but dark or natural colors usually work better.

Your choice of rod and reel depends on your fishing technique and the type of cover. You may need a stiff baitcasting rod and 14-pound mono for fishing in dense brush or vertically jigging with a vibrating blade. But a light- to medium-power spinning rod works better in most other situations. Big smallmouth can be extremely line-shy, and with a lighter outfit, you can use lighter line.

Inexperienced anglers often make the mistake of using heavy gear regardless of the situation, thinking it is needed to land hefty smallmouth. But if you learn to play the fish properly (pages 86-87), you can land any smallmouth on light gear.

RELEASE any big smallmouth you do not intend to mount. Even prime trophy waters contain a surprisingly low number of large fish, so if you keep the big ones for food, you jeopardize your future fishing.

Tips for Trophy Smallmouth

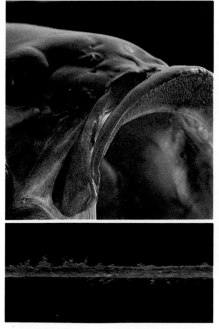

EXAMINE your line often for frays. Most anglers believe that smallmouth cannot damage the line, but the tiny needle-sharp teeth (top) can easily cause fraying (bottom).

SELECT the best-looking spots in the area you intend to fish, then make a few casts in each one. Chances are, a trophy fish will bite right away or not at all. Try the spots again later.

APPROACH a likely spot from deep water. Drift or use your electric motor to get within casting range. If you approach from shallow water, you will probably spook any big smallmouth.

Ice Fishing for Smallmouth

Little has been written about ice fishing for smallmouth bass because most fishermen assume that smallmouth are impossible to catch with the water temperature near freezing. Generally, this is a safe assumption, but in some instances smallmouth bite extremely well through the ice.

In high-competition waters (pages 30-31), smallmouth are usually hungry, so fishing stays good through the winter. In most other waters, anglers may catch an occasional smallmouth, but there is little chance of catching them consistently.

During winter, smallmouth often feed in the same areas where they do in summer. Reefs that top off at 15 feet or less and rocky points with extended lips are top wintertime locations, especially if they adjoin deep water. When smallmouth are feeding, look for them along the edge or on top of the structure at depths of 12 to 20 feet. When not feeding, they move slightly deeper on the same structure or move to small deep-water humps nearby.

DRILL a line of holes along the edge of the structure (dotted line). While one person drills, another clears the holes and measures the depth. After locating the edge of the structure, drill a few more holes at various depths on top of the structure.

MEASURE the depth with a portable flasher. Some fishermen construct a carrying case and use a motorcycle battery for power. The transducer is connected to a rod that holds it in place and keeps it below the surface. A flasher also enables you to detect suspended fish.

Savvy fishermen note precise landmarks in summer so they can easily find their summertime spots after the lake freezes up. Smallmouth under the ice use cover like rocks and logs, just as they do in summer. This explains why one hole sometimes produces almost all the fish.

The best way to pinpoint a good area is to drill a lot of holes, then jig a few minutes in each one. Keep your lure within 18 inches of bottom. If smallmouth are going to strike, they usually strike right away, so it does not pay to wait them out.

Another way to locate smallmouth is to scatter tip-ups at different depths on the structure. Bait up with small minnows. Wind tip-ups may work better than standard tip-ups because they keep the bait moving.

Smallmouth fight hard despite the near-freezing water, so you will need fairly heavy line. Use 20-pound dacron with an 8- to 10-pound mono leader on your tip-ups. Use 6- to 8-pound mono on your jigging rod. The rod should be about 3 feet long and flexible enough to absorb the shock of a sudden run. Be sure your reel has a reliable drag.

A smallmouth often dislodges the lure by thrashing its head on the side of the hole. You will lose fewer fish by drilling a large hole, 8 to 10 inches in diameter, and flaring the bottom (see below).

LURES AND BAITS for ice fishing include: (1) size 3 Jigging Rapala® in perch or silver finish, (2) ice flies with size 6 to 8 hooks. Bait your ice fly with (3) 2 or 3 EuroLarvae™ or (4) a waxworm. For tip-up fishing, use a (5) 2- to 3-inch minnow with a size 4 to 6 hook.

FLARE the bottom of your hole using an ice chisel. With the chisel at an angle and the flat side up, chip away the bottom edge of the entire hole. This way, you can guide your fish into the hole much easier, and the lure is not as likely to be knocked loose against the ice.

SWEEP your fish away from the hole by placing your hand under it and tossing it to the side. If possible, have someone help you. Smallmouth often thrash violently in the hole, throwing the hook at the last moment. By moving quickly, you can save many of these fish.

Index

A

Above-water indicators, 44,45
Abutments, 137
Aggressiveness of smallmouth, 30, 31, 81, 148, 152
Algae, 26, 76, 147
Aluminum canoes, 14
Aluminum semi-V boats, 13, 14
Anchoring, 85, 135, 144, 152
  Jigging and, 92, 145
Anchors, 14, 84
Anti-reverse disengagement button, 9, 10
Artificial lures, 10, 23, 31, 83, 88
  Clear water, 147
  Colors, 89, 91, 95, 109, 127, 146, 147, 153
  Flies, 108-111
  Ice fishing, 155
  Jigging lures, 96, 97
  Jigs, 90-95
  Night fishing, 148
  Plugs, 99-103
  Selecting, 29, 31, 81, 88, 99, 146, 147, 150
  Soft plastics, 112, 113
  Spinners, 104-107
  Techniques for fishing, 88-113, 134, 146, 149
Attractors added to baits and lures, 107, 123
Attractors, fish shelters, 62, 136, 137

B

Backreeling technique, 87
Backtrolling, 13, 83, 93, 121
  Depth control, 83
  Semi-V boats for, 13, 14
Backwater areas in big rivers, 68
Bait, see: Artificial lures, Live bait
Baitcasting gear,
  Reels, 9, 10
  Rods, 9
  Selecting, for various situations, 97, 99, 101, 105, 112, 128, 134, 153
Baitfish, 26, 55
  Lures to imitate, 108, 109
  Smallmouth diet, 26, 28, 34, 46, 49, 51, 62, 128, 149, 151
  Surface activity, 44
  See also: Live bait, Specific kinds of baitfish
Bait-saver tabs, 121, 123
Barometric pressure, 33
Bass boats, 12, 13
Bass bugs, 29, 110, 111, 127, 134, 143
Bays, 52, 56, 57
Beaver lodges, 132-134
Big rivers, 68, 69, 141, 146
  See also: Rivers
Black bass, 20, 37
Black light, 149
Bluegill, 37
  Habitat preferences, 25
  Senses, 23
Bluffs, 45
Boat control, 13, 82-85, 93, 147
Boats, 12-15
  Bass, 12, 13
  Canoes, 13-15, 71, 144
  Jon, 13-15, 141, 144
  Semi-V, 13, 14, 144
  See also: Outboard motors, Trolling motors
Bobbers, slip-, 85, 119, 122, 138, 143, 148
Bog stain, 55
Boron rods, 8
Bottom-fishing techniques, 26, 37, 120

Rocks and boulders, 138, 139
Snaggy bottoms, 10, 107
Spawning, 27
Structure and, 44
Weeds and, 47, 128
Bottom types, 44, 45
  Lakes, 50, 51, 55, 58
  Mid-depth reservoirs, 61
  Pits, 59
  Rivers, 66-69
  Spawning, 27, 37, 38
  Weeds and, 47, 128
Boulders, techniques for fishing, 80, 92, 101, 104, 105, 109, 123, 129, 143, 144
Boundary Waters Canoe Area Wilderness, 71
Bowl-shaped lakes, 58
Breaklines,
  Drifting, 84
  Jigging, 92
  Lakes, 52, 56, 58
  Mid-depth reservoirs, 62
Bridge pilings, big rivers, 69, 142
Bronzeback, 20
Brown bass, 20
Brush, 27
  Flooded, 133
  Lures for fishing, 92, 93, 96, 107, 112, 113
  Techniques for fishing, 80, 152
  See also: Timber and brush
Brush clamp, 135
Brushguard hooks, 130, 134, 135
Brushguard jigs, 93, 129, 134, 135
Brush piles, 133, 143
Bucktail jigs, 93
Bucktail streamers, 108
Bulging the surface, 105
Bugs, see: Bass bugs
Bullet head jigs, 93, 145
Bullheads, 76
  Habitat preferences, 25
Bulrushes, 45, 47, 50, 52
  Techniques for fishing, 101, 106, 129
Buoys, 137
Buzzbaits, 106, 107, 148

C

Cabbage, 53
  Techniues for fishing, 92, 130
California, northern reservoirs, 77
Cam-action hook, 123
Canada waterweed, 131
Canoes, 13-15, 71, 144
Canyon reservoirs, 65, 77
Carp, 76
Casting, 102, 126, 127, 142
  Backhand, 135
  Flippin', 135
  Fly fishing technique, 110, 111, 142
  Forehand, 135
  Lining up targets, 97
  Live bait, 109, 120
  Lob-casting, 120, 123
  Lures, 92, 96, 99-101, 105-107
  Object fishing, 80, 101, 104, 105
  Rods, 8, 9
  Side casting, 142
  Techniques, 92, 97, 110, 111, 135, 138, 147
  Underhand, 135
Catch-and-release fishing, 21, see also: Releasing smallmouth
Catfish, senses of, 23
Cattails, 45, 47, 128
Cemeteries, 136, 137
Chains (anchor), 84, 142
Chameleon effect of smallmouth, 21

Channels, 69, 136
  submerged, 61, 64
Chara, 131
Chest waders, 17
Chubs, 115
Chuggers, 99, 101, 129
Clarity, see: Water clarity
Clear water, 23, 26, 43, 49
  Bass color, 21
  Cold fronts, 33
  Importance of boat control, 82
  Line for fishing, 10
  Lures for fishing, 96, 99, 101, 107
  Night fishing, 81, 147, 148
  Techniques for fishing, 147
Cloud cover, 32, 146
Coal pits, fishing in, 59
Cofilament line, 11
Cold fronts, 31, 33, 141
  Baits and lures for fishing, 91, 115
Cold water,
  Baits and lures for fishing, 99, 115
  Smallmouth dormancy, 24, 28
  Techniques for fishing, 91, 100
  See also: Fall, Ice fishing, Winter
Color selectors, electronic, 16, 89
Colors of lures and rigs, 89, 91, 95, 109, 127, 146, 147, 153
  Murky water, 146
  Ultra-clear water, 147
Competition among smallmouth, 23, 27, 30, 31, 51, 55, 151
  Aggressive behavior and, 30, 31, 81
  Ice fishing, 28, 31, 154
  Live bait fishing and, 91, 115
  Smallmouth and other species, 27, 31, 46, 50
Cone sinker rig, 112, 130, 134
Coontail, 131
Corkie, 123
Countdown technique, 101, 107, 137
Cover, 46, 47, 51, 53, 55, 59
  Canyon reservoirs, 65
  Ice fishing, 155
  Rocks and boulders, 138, 139
  Woody, 133-135
  See also: Specific cover types
Covered docks, 137
Crankbaits, 29, 100, 101, 115
  Attaching, 101
  Casting, 100, 102, 103
  Depth, 100, 101
  Selecting, 29, 31
  Techniques for fishing, 83, 131, 138, 143, 144, 146, 147
  Tuning, 101
  When to use, 130, 146, 147
  See also: Plugs
Crappie, senses of, 23
Crawlers, 99, 101, 103, 148
Crayfish, 116
  Bottom type and, 26, 50, 55, 136
  Hooking technique, 121-123
  Smallmouth diet, 26, 28, 29, 46, 49, 51, 61, 116, 128, 150
  Techniques for fishing, 49, 116, 143
  Tipping lures, 94
Crayfish flies, 109, 143
Creek chubs, 115
Creeks, 27, 56, 61, 62, 141
Crickets, 118
  Hooking technique, 123
Crosswinds, 34
Current, 26, 34, 57, 62, 66-69, 82
  Drifting, slipping and hovering, 84
  Lures for fishing, 93, 107, 108, 110, 111
  Techniques for fishing, 108, 109
  See also: Rivers, Streams

D

Dabbling, 11, 135
Dace, 115
Dams, 67, 77, 144
Daytime fishing, moon phase, 35
Deep water, 26, 49, 81, 126
  Clarity, 147
  Flashers and graph recorders, 16
  Lakes, 51, 54, 55, 58
  Line, 93
  Lures for fishing, 92, 93, 96, 97, 99, 101,
    104, 106, 107, 109, 113, 127, 143, 147
  Oxygen level, 25, 49, 58
  Reservoirs and pits, 59, 61, 65, 74
  River fishing, 67, 141
  Techniques for fishing, 93, 99, 101, 105,
    107, 119
  Trophy smallmouth, 152, 153
  Weeds near, 128, 129
Depth finder, 82, 138
  See also: Flasher, Graph recorder
Dessicants for flies, 110
Detecting strikes, 8, 10, 91, 93, 96, 109, 110,
  112, 115
Diet of smallmouth, 28
Divers, 111, 127, 129, 135, 148, 149
Dobsonfly, 118
Docks, 52, 136, 137
Do-nuthin' rig, 112, 113
Drag, 9, 10, 86, 87, 131
Dragonfly nymphs, 26, 118
Drawdown of reservoirs, 61, 134, 137
Drifting, 84, 138, 142, 143
  Float trips, 145
  Jigging and, 92
  Slowing drift speed, 84, 142
Dropper rigs, 138
Dry flies, 29, 111, 143

E

Eastern rivers region, 75
Eddies, 61, 66-69, 142, 143
  Jigging in, 92
Eels, 94, 115
Egg sinker, 112
Eggs, smallmouth, 37
Electric motors, 82, 84, 93, 152
  Bow-mount, 82
  Canoes, 14, 15
  Transom-mounted, 13-15, 82
Electronic color selectors, 16, 89
Emergent vegetation, 50, 128
  See also: Bulrushes, Cattails
Epilimnion, 26
Equipment, 8-17
  Boats, motors and accessories, 13-15
  Flashers and graph recorders, 16
  Ice fishing, 154, 155
  Rods, reels and line, 9-11
  Waders, 17
EuroLarvae™, 155
Eutrophic lakes, 58, 71, 146

F

Fall, 33, 147
  Baits and lures for fishing, 88, 93, 105,
    115-117, 150
  Lakes, 51-53, 55-58, 72
  Reservoirs, 61, 64, 65, 74, 77
  Rivers, 67, 69, 75, 76
  Smallmouth locations, 44, 45, 49,
    129-131, 141
  Techniques for fishing, 49, 93, 130, 131

Trophy smallmouth, 150, 152
Fall turnover, 49, 51, 55
Fatheads, 115
Feeding, 28, 29, 44
  Cold fronts, 33, 34
  Ice-cover season, 28
  Lakes, 50-53, 57, 58
  Reservoirs, 61-63, 65, 74
  Rivers, 66-69
  Seasonal patterns, 28, 32, 49-51
  Water clarity, 32
  Weather, 32-34
Felt soles for wading gear, 17
Fencelines, 137
Fiberglass canoes, 14
Fiberglass rods, 8
Fiberglass semi-V boats, 13, 14
Fingerlings, 37
Fish attractors, 62, 136, 137
Fish population surveys, 43
Fishing contests, 43, 151
Fishing pressure, 5, 31, 43, 71, 72, 74, 75,
  141, 144, 148, 151
Flashers, 13-16, 44, 141, 154
Flats, 53, 62
Flies, 108-111
  Attaching, 109
  Rods, reels and line, 10, 11, 109-111
  Sizes for smallmouth, 108-111
  Techniques for fishing, 108-111, 127, 129,
    142, 143
  When to use, 127, 129, 134
Flippin', 11, 135
Floatants, paste-type, 110, 111
Float trips, 144, 145
Flooded brush and timber, 47, 67, 133
  Lures for fishing, 93, 96, 97
  Reservoirs, 61-64
  See also: Brush, Timber and brush
Flowages, 64
Fluorescent line, 10, 149
Fluorescent lures and rigs, 89, 146
Foundations, fishing around, 136
Freelining, 119, 123, 134
Frogs, 103, 117, 143, 145
  Hooking techniques, 121, 123
  Techniques for fishing, 143, 145
Fry guarding, 37, 49, 51, 55, 61, 126, 127

G

Gauges, surface temperature, 16
Gear ratio, 9
Gizzard shad, 151
Golden shiners, 115
Gradient of rivers, 141
Graph recorders, 16
Graphite rods, 8, 9, 11, 91
Grasshoppers, 118
  Hooking technique, 123
Gravel bars, 66, 68
Gravel pits, fishing in, 59
Great Lakes region, 70-73
  Manmade features, 136
Green trout, 20
Guarding, see: Fry guarding

H

Habitat preferences, 24-27, 45
  Competition level, 31
  See also: Specific habitats
Hackle-wing streamers, 108
Hearing of fish, 23
Helicoptering, 96, 97, 105, 106, 127, 129
Hellgrammites, 118
  Hooking techniques, 121, 122

Imitations, 109
  Smallmouth diet, 26
  Techniques for fishing, 118, 143
  Tipping jigs, 94
Hip boots, 17, 141
Homing instinct, 38, 39, 49
Hooks,
  Brushguard, 130, 134
  Cam-action, 123
  Fine-wire, 134
  Flattening the barb, 95, 127
  for Soft plastic bait, 112
  Split-shot rigs, 120
  Stinger, 95, 121
  Super Hook, 121
  Trailer, 107
  Weedless, 113, 129
Hovering, 84
  Vertical jigging and, 93
Humps,
  Lakes, 50-52, 57
  Reservoirs, 61, 63, 64
  Sand-gravel, 53
Hybridization of bass, 20

I

Ice chisel, 155
Ice fishing, 31, 154, 155
  Baits, lures and rigs, 97, 155
Insects,
  as Bait, 118
  Smallmouth diet, 26, 28, 29, 50, 51, 55, 66,
    67, 109, 118, 128, 133, 151
  See also: Specific insects
Iron ore pits, 59
Islands, 54, 57, 69, 72

J

Jetties, 136
Jigging flies, 108, 127, 129, 134, 135
Jigging Lures, 96, 97
  Attaching, 97
  Ice fishing, 155
  Rod and line recommendations, 97
  Techniques for fishing, 92-95
  See also: Jigging spoons, Tailspins,
    Vibrating blades
Jigging minnows, 97, 155
Jigs, 29, 91-95, 100
  Bicolor heads, 95
  Brushguard, 93, 129, 130, 134, 135
  Colors of, 91
  Dressing, 92, 93
  Flattening hook barb, 95
  Floating, 138, 143
  Head styles, 92, 93
  Rods, reels and line for fishing, 91
  Slow-sinking, 92, 127
  Soft-plastic baits on jig heads, 112, 113
  Techniques for fishing, 91-95, 127, 129, 130,
    134, 135, 137, 138, 143-146
  Tin heads, 92, 127
  Tipping, 91, 92, 94, 95, 127
  Trolling, 92, 93
  Weight recommendations, 92, 93, 127, 129,
    138, 144
  When to use, 146-148
Jigging spoons, 96, 97, 134
Jon boats, 13-15, 141, 144

K

Keeper-style jig heads, 112, 113

Knots,
   Attaching flies, 109
   Minnow plugs, 103

L

Lake Erie, 73
Lake Huron, 72
Lake Michigan, 72
Lake Ontario, 73
Lakes,
   Bowl-shaped, 58
   Eutrophic, 58, 71, 146
   Fertile, 26, 151
   Mesotrophic, 50-53, 71, 128
   Midwestern region, 76
   Northern natural, 70, 71
   Oligotrophic, 54-57, 71, 128
   Smallmouth location in, 24, 26, 38, 49
   See also: Great Lakes region
Lampreys, 115
Landing smallmouth, 87
Largemouth bass, 20-23, 26, 74
   Appearance compared to smallmouth,
      20, 21
   Competition with smallmouth, 27, 31, 46, 50
   Fishing for, compared to smallmouth, 81,
      88, 91, 99, 104, 107, 112
   Habitat preferences, 25-27, 37, 47, 58, 61,
      64, 81, 128, 133
   Senses, 23
Larval insects, see: Insects
Lateral-line sense, 23, 96
Latitudes,
   Growth rates and, 29
   Spawning dates and, 126
Leaders,
   Clear water, 147
   Fly fishing, 109
   Steel, 99
Lead-head jigs, see: Jigs
Leech flies, 109, 143
Leeches, 116
   Carrying, 122
   Hooking techniques, 121-123
   Techniques for fishing, 143
   Tipping lures, 94, 107, 127
   When to use, 127
Light levels, 32, 33, 45, 49
   Clear water, 147
   Onshore winds, 34
   Rough water, 34
   See also: Shade
Lighthouse foundations, 69, 136
Lightning, 33
Lily pads, 47, 131
Line, 10, 11
   Abrasion-resistant, 128, 134, 138
   Dacron, 155
   Diameter, 11, 146
   Floating, 10, 109
   Fluorescent, 10, 149
   Fly fishing, 10, 11, 109-111
   Ice fishing, 155
   Light, 10, 102, 119, 152
   Low-stretch, 93
   Selecting, 8-11, 91, 93, 97, 99-102, 105, 109,
      112, 123, 128, 146, 147, 152, 153
   Sinking, 109
   Sink-tip, 10, 109
   Stretch factor, 10, 93
   Trophy smallmouth, 153
   Visibility, 10, 11
Lip-landing, 87
Liquid-crystal recorders (LCRs), 16
Lithium battery, 148
Live Bait, 114-123
   Competition and, 31

Disadvantages, 115
Keeping alive, 115-118, 122
Rods, reels and line for, 8, 9, 119
Size for smallmouth, 81, 115-117, 150
during Spawning, 127
Techniques for fishing, 83, 119-123, 130, 134,
   135
Tipping with, 91, 92, 94, 95, 107, 129
Trophy smallmouth, 150
When to use, 115, 127, 134, 147
See also: Specific types of live bait
Live-rubber skirt, 123
Lob-casting, 120, 123
Logjams, 67, 142, 143, 145
Logs, 133
   Techniques for fishing, 80, 92, 109, 123, 129
Low-clarity water, 26, 49, 146
   Bass color, 21
   Big rivers, 68
   Cold fronts, 33
   Line for fishing, 10
   Lures for fishing, 89, 91, 96, 101
   Spawning and, 27
   Techniques for fishing, 93, 146
Lures, see: Artificial lures

M

Madtoms, 115
Manmade features, 136, 137
Marabou streamers, 108
Marinas, 43, 44, 68
Meanmouth bass, 20
Medium-sized rivers, 66, 67, 141
   See also: Rivers, Streams
Mending the line, 108
Mesotrophic lakes, 50-53, 71, 128
Micropterus dolomieui (smallmouth bass), 20
Mid-depth reservoirs, 60-63, 74
Midwestern rivers region, 76
Mid-south reservoir region, 74
Milfoil, 131
Milt, 37
Mining pits, 59
Minnow buckets, 115, 122
Minnow plugs, 29, 99, 100, 129
   Attaching, 100, 103
   Size for smallmouth, 88
   Techniques for fishing, 100, 103, 127, 129,
     134, 143
   Tuning, 101
   When to use, 147, 148
   See also: Plugs
Minnows, 115
   Hooking techniques, 121-123
   Lures to imitate, 96, 100, 110, 111
   Smallmouth diet, 50, 66, 67
   Techniques for fishing, 115, 155
   Tipping lures, 94, 95, 107
   See also: Baitfish, Live bait, Specific types
     of minnows
Monofilament line, see: Line
Moon phase, 35
Motors, 12-15
   Boat control, 82
   Canoes, 14, 15
   Drifting with, 84
   Electric, 82, 84, 93, 152
   Outboard, 12, 82, 141, 144
   Selecting, 12-15
Mouth size on smallmouth, 21
Mudline, 34
Mudminnows, 115
Mummichogs, 115
Municipal treatment plants, 143
Murky water, see: Low-clarity water

N

Nest guarding, 37, 126, 127, 150
   Lakes, 51, 55
   Mid-depth reservoirs, 61
   See also: Spawning
Nests,
   Lakes, 50, 51, 54, 58
   Locating, 126, 127
   Mid-depth reservoirs, 61
   Small to medium-sized rivers, 66
   Water depth, 37
   See also: Spawning
Nightcrawlers, 116
   Hooking techniques, 121, 122
   Techniques for fishing, 116, 138, 143
   Tipping lures, 94, 107
Night fishing, 16, 74, 147-149
   Lures, 88, 99, 101, 104, 105, 107, 148, 150
   Moon phase, 35
   Techniques, 147-149
   Trophy smallmouth, 150
Noise and spooking smallmouth, 23, 85,
   147, 152
Northern California reservoirs, 77
Northern natural lakes region, 70, 71
Northern pike, 54, 71
   Competition with smallmouth, 27, 31, 46, 50
   Habitat preferences, 25
   Senses, 23
Nylon wading gear, 17
Nymphs, 29, 109, 110, 142, 143

O

Object fishing, 80, 101, 104, 105
Oligotrophic lakes, 54-57, 71, 128
Onshore winds, 34
Oswego bass, 20
Outboard motors, 12, 82, 141, 144
Oxygen levels, 24, 25, 49, 58

P

Pacific northwest, 77
Panfish, 37
pH, 25
pH meters, 16
Pilings, big rivers, 68, 69, 142
Pits, 59
Plastic worms, 112, 113, 127, 129
Playing smallmouth, 10, 86, 87, 97, 153
Plug knocker, 138
Plugs, 99-103
   Attaching, 99-101, 103
   Rods, reels and line, 99-101
   Size, 88, 99
   Techniques for fishing, 99-103
   Tuning, 100, 101
   See also: Specific types of plugs
Points, 45
   Crosswinds, 34
   Ice fishing, 154
   Mesotrophic lakes, 50
   Mid-depth reservoirs, 62, 63
   Rivers, 66
   Slope of, 52, 53, 57
   Spawning, 56
Pools in rivers and streams, 26, 66-69
Poppers, 110, 127
Pork frog, 94, 148
Pork rind, 91, 92, 94, 104, 107, 129
Portaging, 14, 15, 71
Power plants, 143
Predators of smallmouth, 27, 28, 31, 46
Prime smallmouth waters, 70-77
Propbait, 99, 101, 103, 127, 129, 148

Q

Quarries, 59
Quetico Provincial Park, 71

R

Railroad grades, submerged, 136
Rain, 33, 41, 146
Rattles on lures, for murky water, 146
Redeye, 20
Redtail chubs, 115
Reefs,
  Anchoring near, 85
  Crankbait casting, 100, 102
  Crosswinds, 34
  Great Lakes region, 72
  Ice fishing, 154
  Lakes, 53, 56, 57
  Reservoirs, 64
  Shade and, 46
Reels, 8-11
  Anti-reverse disengagement button, 9, 10
  Baitcasting, 9
  Drag on, 9, 10
  Fly-fishing, 10
  Gear ratio, 9
  Level-wind, 11
  Selecting, 8-11, 99, 101, 105, 153
  Single-action, 10
  Spinning, 8, 9
Releasing smallmouth, 5, 39, 87, 95, 127, 153
Reservoirs,
  Canyon, 65, 77
  Clear water, 147
  Eastern rivers region, 75
  Manmade features, 136, 137
  Mid-depth, 60-63
  Mid-South region, 27, 74
  Northern California, 77
  Shallow, 64, 74, 77
  Smallmouth location, 27, 38
  Southwestern, 77
  Techniques for fishing, 136, 137
  Trophy smallmouth, 151
  Woody cover, 133, 134
Retrieves,
  Do-nuthin', 112
  Jigging, 91-93, 112
  Stop-and-go, 89, 100
  Twitch-and-pause, 99, 110, 111
  Ribbon leech, 116
Rigs,
  Cone sinker, 112, 130, 134
  Dropper, 138
  Ice fishing, 154, 155
  Slip-bobber, 85, 119, 122, 138, 143, 148
  Slip-sinker, 119, 121, 130, 143, 145
  Snag-resistant, 112, 113, 130, 138
  Soft-plastic baits, 112, 113, 127
  Split-shot, 119-121, 129, 134, 138, 143
  Texas-style, 112, 113, 127
  3-way swivel, 99, 145
Riprap, 68, 69, 143
Rivers,
  Baits and lures for fishing, 109, 115, 117, 142, 143
  Big, 68, 69, 141, 146
  Boats for fishing, 14, 15, 141, 144
  Eastern region, 75
  Gradient, 141
  Mid-South region, 74
  Midwestern region, 76
  Northern region, 70
  Pacific northwest region, 77
  Smallmouth locations, 49, 141
  Small to medium-sized, 66, 67
  Southwestern region, 77

Techniques for fishing, 49, 84, 109, 110, 133, 141-145
  When to fish, 141
  See also: Current, Streams
Roadbeds, submerged, 63, 136
Rocks and boulders, 45, 46, 54, 55, 59, 62, 64, 92, 138, 139
Rocky bottom, 26
  Rod and line recommendations for fishing, 8, 10
  Techniques for fishing, 122
  See also: Bottom types
Rods, 8-11
  Baitcasting, 8, 97, 99, 101, 105, 112, 128, 134, 153
  Boron, 8
  Casting, 9
  Fiberglass, 8
  Fly-fishing, 10, 109-111
  Graphite, 8, 9, 11, 91
  Length recommendations, 8, 9, 139
  Live bait fishing, 9, 119
  Playing smallmouth, 86, 87, 139
  Selecting, 8-11
  Spinning, 8, 91, 99, 101, 105, 107, 112, 128, 153
  Trolling, 9
  Trophy smallmouth, 153
Rubber bands, hooking live bait, 122
Rubber wading gear, 17

S

Salamanders, see: Spring lizards, Waterdogs
Salmon, 71, 72, 77
Sandgrass, 53, 131
Sauger, senses of, 23
Scent products, 23
Scouting for smallmouth in winter, 49
Sea anchor, 84
Seasonal movement of smallmouth, 44, 49-69, 127, 152
Seawalls, 136
Semi-V boats, 13, 14, 144
Senses, 22, 23
Setting the hook, 8, 10, 86, 87, 91, 111, 116, 120-123
Shade, 44-47, 65, 80, 92, 133
  See also: Light levels
Shadows, spooking fish with, 23, 81, 152
Shad, 61, 74, 115, 151
Shallow reservoirs, 64, 74, 77
Shallow water, 25, 26, 49
  Boats for, 15
  Flashers and graph recorders, 16
  Lakes, 51, 54
  Lures and rigs for fishing, 92, 99, 104-107, 110, 120, 121, 127, 143
  Techniues for fishing, 92, 93, 99, 101, 103-105, 107, 109, 119, 133, 146
  Night fishing, 148
  Reservoirs, 61, 65, 74
  River fishing, 67, 141
  Weather and, 33, 49
  Shiners, 29, 115, 122, 149
Ship channels, 136
Shipwrecks, 136
Shocking surveys, 43, 77
Shorelines, 58, 62, 100
Side-casting, 142
Silt load in rivers, 68, 76, 141
Single-spin spinnerbait, 106
Sink-tip line, 109
Sinkers, 99, 138, 139
Skating dry flies, 111
Skirt, live rubber, 123
Sliders, 111

Slip-bobber rig, 122
  Hooking baits, 122
  Lighted for night fishing, 148
  Techniques for fishing, 122, 143
  When to use, 119, 122, 138
Slip-sinker rig, 121, 130
  Hooking baits, 121
  Techniques for fishing, 121, 143, 145
  When to use, 119
Slipping, 84, 144
Sloughs, 68
Smallmouth bass,
  Color phase, 21, 37
  Common names, 20
  Description, 20, 21
  Growth rates, 28, 29
  Habitat preferences, 16, 24-29
  Hybrids, 20
  Lifespan, 28
  Range, 20, 21, 28, 48, 49, 70
  Schooling behavior, 26, 49, 51, 55, 69, 81, 93
  Senses, 23
  Size, 28, 29, 71, 72, 74, 75, 77, 81
  Stocking, 20, 70, 75, 77
  World record, 21
Small rivers, 66, 67
  See also: Rivers, Streams
Smell, 23
Soft-shelled crayfish, 115, 116
Soft-plastic dressings on jigs, 91-93, 95
Soft-plastic lures, 112, 113, 127, 134
Soil composition, 45
Southwestern reservoirs, 77
Spawning, 37, 44, 49, 126, 127, 129
  Baits and lures for fishing, 89, 91, 99, 105, 127, 150
  Dates for by latitude, 126
  Lakes, 50-58
  Habitat, 27, 37, 38
  Homing and, 38, 39
  Pits, 59
  Reservoirs, 61, 62, 64, 65, 136
  Rivers, 66-69
  Techniques for fishing 16, 126, 127
  Trophy smallmouth 150, 151
  Water temperature, 37, 49, 50, 54, 55
Spinnerbaits, 104-107, 127
  Rods, reels and line for fishing, 105
  Size for smallmouth, 88, 104, 105, 127, 148
  Techniques for fishing, 104, 105, 107, 127, 129, 130, 134, 143, 145
  When to use, 104-106, 127, 130, 134, 146, 148
Spinner rigs, 123
Spinners, see: Buzzbaits, Spinnerbaits, Standard spinners, Weight-forward spinners
Spinning gear,
  Reels, 8, 9, 87, 112, 128
  Rods, 8, 9, 87
  Selecting, for various situations, 101, 105, 107, 112, 119, 128, 153
Split-shot rigs, 120, 138
  Hooking baits, 121
  Techniques for fishing, 120, 143
  When to use, 119, 129, 134
Spooking fish, 23, 81, 84, 85, 99, 111, 133, 134, 152
Spotted bass, 27, 141
  Appearance, compared to smallmouth, 20, 21
  Senses, 23
Spring, 33, 45, 49, 130, 133, 151
  Lakes, 50, 51, 54, 55
  Lures for fishing, 105
  Reservoirs, 61-64, 74, 77
  Rivers, 66, 68, 69, 75, 76
  Smallmouth locations, 137
  See also: Spawning

Spring lizard, 117
  Hooking technique, 121
  When to use, 127
Springs, 67, 76
Standard spinners, 105-107
  Attaching, 107
  Size for smallmouth, 107, 145
  Techniques for fishing, 105-107, 143, 145
  Tipping with live bait, 107
  When to use, 89, 105, 127
Stickbaits, 99, 101, 147
Stinger hook, 95
Stocking of smallmouth, 20, 70, 75, 77
Stop-and-go retrieve, 89, 100
Storms, 33, 51, 141, 147
Streamers, 108, 109, 127, 143
Streams, 33, 43, 147, 152
  Equipment for fishing, 17
  Slipping and hovering, 84
  Smallmouth location in, 24, 26, 38, 49, 133
  Spawning in, 27, 49, 65, 66
  Techniques for fishing, 92
  See also: Current, Rivers
Stretch factor in line, 10
Structure, 44, 45, 50-69
  Ice fishing, 154
  Jigging and, 92
  Lakes, 50-58
  Night fishing, 148
  Pits, 59
  Reservoirs, 61-65
  Rivers, 66-69
  Stumps, 47, 61, 64, 69, 133
  Techniques for fishing, 80, 101, 104-106, 143
Sub-surface plugs, 99
  See also: Crankbaits, Minnow plugs,
    Vibrating plugs
Surface plugs, 99, 129, 134
  See also: Chuggers, Crawlers, Propbaits,
    Stickbaits
Summer, 33, 44, 45, 49, 118, 129-131
  Baits for fishing, 116, 118
  Lakes, 51-53, 55, 57, 58, 72
  Reservoirs, 61-65, 74, 76, 77, 147
  Rivers, 66-69, 75
  Smallmouth locations, 131, 137
  Techniques for fishing, 81, 93, 115, 116
  Trophy smallmouth, 152
  See also: Warm water
Sunfish family, 20
Surface-temperature gauge, 16
Swivels, 145, 147
  Ball-bearing, 107
  Snap swivel, 97, 99
  Three-way rig, 99

T

Tailspins, 96, 97
Tandem spinnerbait, 106
Target casting, see: Object fishing
Techniques for fishing, 80-123, 146
  Artificial lures, 88-113
  Boat control, 82-85
  Bottom-fishing, 10, 26, 27, 37, 44, 45, 47,
    64, 101, 107, 120, 128, 138-143
  Bulging the surface, 105
  Casting, 92, 97, 102, 103
  Clear water, 147
  Countdown, 101, 107, 137
  Flies, 108-111
  Float trips, 144, 145
  Freelining, 123
  Helicoptering, 96, 97, 105, 106, 127, 129
  Ice fishing, 154, 155
  Jigs, 91-95
  Jig trolling, 92, 93

Live bait, 119-123
Manmade features, 136
Mending the line, 108
Night fishing, 148, 149
Object fishing, 80, 104, 105
Playing a smallmouth, 86, 87
Plugs, 99-103
Rivers, 141-145
Rocks and boulders, 138, 139
Skating flies, 111
Slip-bobber rigs, 122
Slip-sinker rigs, 121
Soft plastics, 112, 113
Spawning, 126, 127
Spinners, 104-107
Split-shot rigs, 120
Trolling, 83
Trophy smallmouth, 151-153
Vertical jigging, 93, 96
Wading, 17, 143, 144
Weeds, 128-131
Woody cover, 133-135
Temperature, see: Water temperature
Temperature gauge, 16
Texas rig for soft plastics, 112, 113, 129,
    130, 134
Thermocline, 49, 58
Tiger salamanders, 117
Tiller steering, 13, 14, 82, 83
Timber, 47, 133
  See also: Fallen timber
Timber and brush, 47, 61-65, 133-135
  Lures for fishing, 96
  Rod and line recommendations for fishing,
    8, 10
  Techniques for fishing, 80, 97, 101
  See also: Brush, Flooded brush and timber,
    Stumps
Time of day for fishing, 31, 81, 146
Tin jig heads, 92, 127
Tip-ups, 155
Tippet for dry flies, 111
Trailer-hook attractor, 107
Tributaries, 66, 68, 77
Trolling, 9, 83, 138
  Backtrolling, 13, 83, 93, 121
  Long-line, 100
  Lures and rigs, 92, 93, 96, 99, 121
  Rods and reels, 8, 9
  Techniques, 100, 138, 143
Trophy smallmouth, 72, 74, 88, 116, 151-153
  Baits and lures, 88, 99, 116, 117, 150
Trout, 54, 71, 72, 76, 77
  Habitat preferences, 25, 26
Tuffies, 115
Turnover, see: Fall turnover

U

Ultraviolet light, 149

V

Vertical jigging, 93, 96
Vibrating blades, 96, 97, 146, 153
Vibrating plugs, 101
  Attaching, 101
  Rattle chamber for murky water, 89
  Techniques for fishing, 101
  When to use, 89, 146
Vision of fish, 23

W

Waders, 17, 141
  Boot-foot model vs. stocking-foot model, 17
Wading, 17, 143, 144

Walleye, 54, 71, 72, 91
  Habitat preferences, 25, 81, 141
  Senses, 23, 32
Warm water,
  Baits for fishing, 116
  Smallmouth preference, 24, 42-47
  Techniques for fishing, 91, 100
  See also: Summer
Water clarity, 26, 75
  Bass color, 21
  Colors of lures and rigs, 89
  Effect on feeding, 32, 33, 50
Water temperature, 24, 25, 49
  Homing, 38
  Lakes, 26, 50, 51, 54, 55, 58
  Live bait fishing, 115, 116
  Plugs, 99
  Preferences of fish, 25
  Reservoirs, 61, 64
  Rivers, 67-69
  Size of smallmouth and, 24
  Smallmouth location, 26, 38, 49-51
  Spawning, 37, 49, 50, 54, 55
  Trophy smallmouth, 152
Waterdogs, 117, 121
  Hooking technique, 121
  When to use, 127
Waxworm, 155
Weather, 32-34, 146, 147
  Barometric pressure, 33
  Competition level and, 31
  Effect on smallmouth activity, 32-34, 49, 51,
    54, 61, 141, 146, 147
  Rain, 33, 41, 146
  See also: Cold fronts
Weedless hooks, 113, 129
Weeds, 27, 33, 46, 47, 81
  Eutrophic lakes, 58
  Lures for fishing, 92, 100, 106, 112, 113
  Mesotrophic lakes, 53, 128
  Oligotrophic lakes, 55
  Pits, 59
  Reservoirs, 64
  Rod and line recommendations for fishing,
    10, 128
  Techniques for fishing, 26, 33, 128-131
Weight-forward spinner, 106, 107
Weight-forward tapers, 109
White bass, 44
Wild celery, 47, 131
Wilderness areas, 15, 71
Willow cats, 115
Wind, 33, 34, 50, 51, 146, 147
  Anchoring, 85
  Boat control, 82-85
  Current and, 26, 34
  Drifting and, 84
  Fishing in bulrushes, 129
  Lures for fishing in, 93
Wind tip-ups, 155
Wingdams, 69
Winter, 38, 49, 154, 155
  Lakes, 51-55, 57, 58
  Reservoirs, 61-65, 77
  Rivers, 66-69, 141
  Techniques for fishing, 93, 143
  See also: Cold water, Ice fishing
Woody cover, 52, 133-135
  Techniques for fishing, 133-135
  See also: Brush, Timber and brush, Stumps
Worm blower, 138
Worm oil, 112

Y

Yarn as attractor, 123
Yellow perch, senses of, 23